What We Owe Each Other: Morality, Liberty, Markets, and Meaning in a Modern World

How Adam Smith and Ludwig von Mises Still Shape the Choices That Shape Our Lives

Francis Williams

What We Owe Each Other: Morality, Liberty, Markets, and Meaning in a Modern World

Cover Design: Author
First Edition
ISBN: 978-1-0694241-6-7
Printed in USA

"Liberty means responsibility.
That is why most men dread it."

~ George Bernard Shaw

We don't need to agree on everything to
live in peace,
we only need to agree
not to force each other to agree.

Freedom is not a loophole -
it's a responsibility we give to each
other, day by day, choice by choice.

To the people of the world -
who understand that freedom is
not easy,
not guaranteed,
and never free -
but choose it anyway.

This is for you.

And to my children,
and my children's children -

May you live free.

Always.

Disclaimer

This book is a work of nonfiction and philosophical interpretation. While it draws upon the historical writings and ideas of Adam Smith and Ludwig von Mises, it is not a direct representation of their full works or views. The interpretations, reflections, and conclusions presented herein are those of the author and are intended to offer a modern, accessible synthesis of classical liberal thought.

This book is not intended to serve as legal, economic, or political advice. Readers are encouraged to consult primary sources, qualified professionals, and diverse perspectives when forming their own views on public policy, economics, or ethics.

All efforts have been made to ensure accuracy and clarity. However, the author and publisher disclaim any liability for any errors, omissions, or interpretations contained in this book or for any consequences arising from its use.

Any resemblance to actual persons or organizations is purely coincidental unless explicitly stated.

Note to Readers

This book was written with the assistance of advanced artificial intelligence tools, which were used to help research, organize, and refine the structure and language of the text. These tools served as collaborative instruments - supporting ideation, synthesizing complex historical sources, and enhancing clarity - while the author remained fully responsible for the book's direction, voice, and final content.

All interpretations, arguments, and philosophical positions reflect the author's intent and worldview. The use of AI is acknowledged as part of a modern writing process that combines human creativity with technological innovation.

The goal, as always, is to make meaningful ideas more accessible, engaging, and relevant for today's reader.

Thank you for being part of this conversation.

What We Owe Each Other: Morality, Liberty, Markets, and Meaning in a Modern World

Table of Contents

Introduction

Why These Old Ideas Matter More Than Ever

You may not know Adam Smith or Ludwig von Mises personally - but by the end of this book, I hope you'll think of them not as distant thinkers on dusty shelves, but as **fellow travelers**. Not prophets. Not ideologues. Just two curious, relentless minds asking the most important question we can ask:

What does it mean to live well and freely among other people?

That question hasn't gone away.

In fact, in today's world - full of distrust, division, censorship, inequality, and economic disorientation - it may be more urgent than ever.

We are told we must choose between freedom and morality.
Between progress and tradition.
Between the needs of the individual and the good of the whole.

Smith and Mises show us that these are **false choices**.

They remind us - across centuries and revolutions - that freedom is not a rejection of morality. It is *its best expression*. That cooperation doesn't require control. That progress doesn't need planning. And that prosperity is not just about wealth - but about **trust, dignity, and purpose.**

Adam Smith, writing in the 18th century, saw clearly that **morality and markets are not enemies**. His lesser-known book, *The Theory of Moral Sentiments*, is a profound exploration of why we care about each other - even when no one is watching. In it, he shows how our conscience is shaped not by laws, but by sympathy, social experience, and the desire to be "lovely" - that is, *worthy of love.*

His later work, *The Wealth of Nations*, revealed how free trade, when grounded in voluntary action and protected by justice, could generate more peace and prosperity than any monarch or master planner ever could. For

1

Smith, morality wasn't something to be added to capitalism - it was **its moral foundation**.

Ludwig von Mises, writing in the 20th century, picked up that moral thread. He made the case that **human action is purposeful, not random** - and that every individual, regardless of status, makes choices based on what they believe will improve their life. In recognizing this, Mises defended not only markets, but human dignity itself.

He warned that when governments try to override these personal decisions - by central planning, forced equality, or utopian coercion - they don't create justice. They create **dependence, stagnation, and tyranny**.

Together, Smith and Mises offer us something rare: a worldview where **freedom and morality are not at war**, but in harmony - where economics is not cold or clinical, but personal, even sacred. Their ideas have survived centuries not because they are trendy, but because **they are true**.

And yet, in our time, we seem to be forgetting them.

We chase equality without asking at what cost to liberty.
We invoke justice without clarity or humility.
We fear freedom because we no longer trust each other to use it well.

That's why this book exists.

Not to romanticize the past - but to bring the **best of the past into our present**, and make it live again.

What follows is not a textbook or a treatise. It's a **conversation** - with you, with the world around us, and with the two great thinkers whose moral courage and clarity still light the way forward.

If you've ever felt that liberty is more than a slogan…
That morality matters more than ideology…
And that a better society cannot be forced but must be *chosen* -
Then this book is for you.

Let's rediscover the ideas that helped build the most free and flourishing societies in history.

Let's bring them into the 21st century - not to preserve them, but to **practice them**.

Because the world does not need new truths.

It needs the **courage to remember old ones** - and the wisdom to live them well.

PART I:

THE MORAL ROOTS OF A FREE SOCIETY

Chapter 1: The Mirror Within

Sympathy, Empathy, and the Birth of Morality

I want to start with something so ordinary it's almost invisible: a sigh. Not your sigh. Someone else's. Maybe a stranger sitting beside you on the subway, or a coworker across the break room. You don't know what caused it - fatigue, disappointment, maybe something deeper. And yet, when you hear it, something in you moves. You glance up. You feel a tug - not from logic, not from duty, but from somewhere quieter and older. That moment, as fleeting as it is, holds the key to understanding how human beings form morality - not by commandment, not by calculation, but by connection.

Adam Smith, the so-called father of capitalism, began not with gold or markets but with this: sympathy. Or, as we'd say today, *empathy*. In *The Theory of Moral Sentiments*, he posited that human beings are not isolated atoms of self-interest but deeply interwoven observers of each other's joy and suffering. Before he ever wrote about wealth, he wrote about the invisible threads of emotion, perception, and judgment that bind us.

This idea - radical in its subtlety - transformed how I understand ethics and society. Because if you can see the world through another person's eyes, even for a second, you've taken the first step toward justice. Toward trust. Toward civilization.

But let me back up.

Sympathy Is the Starting Point

Smith didn't mean sympathy in the Hallmark-card sense. He meant something closer to what psychologists today call *affective empathy*: the ability to feel, or at least imagine, another's emotion by placing ourselves in their situation. We do this instinctively. When we watch a toddler trip and fall, we flinch. When we hear someone tell a painful story, we wince, even if it's fictional. When our friend laughs until they cry, we smile reflexively. These moments, trivial as they may seem, form the lattice of moral life.

They're also ancient.

We evolved in tight-knit tribes where survival depended not just on strength or cunning but on *synchronization*. If someone spotted danger, others had to recognize it - and fast. Our brains adapted. Mirror neurons fired. We learned to read each other, to intuit emotion from tone and posture and breath. Over time, these faculties became not just tools for coordination but the raw material for *judgment*.

And that's where Smith goes deeper than most modern theories. He didn't stop at the observation that we feel for others. He asked: *What happens inside us when we try to evaluate whether someone else is feeling what they ought to feel?*

Think about that. When you see someone explode in rage over a minor inconvenience, you don't just observe it - you assess it. You silently ask: *Is this reaction fitting? Reasonable? Proportional?*

This internal dialogue, Smith said, is mediated by what he called the **"impartial spectator."** It's like a little judge inside us - not perfectly neutral, but striving to be. When we watch others, and when we imagine others watching us, this spectator evaluates the rightness of actions. It's where conscience is born - not in rules, but in relationships.

The Birth of the Impartial Spectator

Let me give a modern example. Imagine you're in traffic. A car cuts you off, and you instinctively shout something unkind. But then you look over and notice a car seat in the back, and the driver is visibly distraught. Maybe their child is sick. Maybe they're rushing to a hospital. Suddenly, your judgment softens.

What changed?

Your impartial spectator entered the scene. You imagined their context, their reasons. You didn't condone the behavior, but you *reframed* it. That shift - from anger to perspective - is the engine of human morality.

The spectator doesn't make us saints. But it nudges us toward fairness. It's what allows us to say, "I wouldn't want someone to treat me that way," and mean it. It's what drives everything from apologies to laws to human rights.

And crucially, it develops *within us*, not outside of us. That's a powerful claim. It says that morality doesn't require a sovereign ruler or divine commandment. It arises from our nature as *social beings*.

This insight is the starting point for everything else in this book - because if we are, at root, creatures capable of sympathy and evaluation, then the systems we build (economic, political, educational) must align with that nature - or risk breaking us.

Why This Matters in a Modern World

We live in a time where morality is often shouted from platforms but rarely practiced in public. We cancel. We moralize. We signal virtue but forget to inhabit it. And perhaps worst of all, we increasingly view each other not as individuals with stories and pain, but as members of opposing camps: political, cultural, economic.

In that climate, Smith's impartial spectator is more than a moral curiosity - it's a survival tool.

Because it reminds us that moral judgment is not about tribal allegiance, but about context, proportion, and humanity. It invites us to judge - but only after imagining. To act - but only after reflection.

This is where Mises quietly joins the conversation.

Human Action Begins with the Moral Actor

Ludwig von Mises, the Austrian economist who wrote *Human Action*, would agree with Smith on one crucial point: the individual is the fundamental unit of society. But where Smith explored *why* we care about others, Mises asked: *How do we choose?*

For Mises, all human behavior is intentional. We act to remove felt uneasiness. That is, we see a better state of affairs in our minds, and we act to bring it about. Whether it's buying groceries, starting a business, or helping a friend, the principle is the same: human action is purposeful.

Now combine that with Smith's idea.

If we are both *moral observers* and *rational choosers*, then every action we take carries not just economic meaning, but ethical weight. A business decision isn't just about profit - it's about impact. A vote isn't just an expression of preference - it's a statement of judgment. A conversation isn't just exchange - it's a moral encounter.

You begin to see why these thinkers, read together, can shape a philosophy of life.

The Morality of the Middle Class

I want to pause here and ground all of this in something real: the modern middle-class reader.

You, reading this now, may be a teacher, a nurse, a manager, a small business owner, a stay-at-home parent. You navigate dozens of decisions every day - how to spend your money, how to treat others, what to support, what to oppose. Some decisions feel tiny. Others feel overwhelming.

What Smith and Mises offer is a kind of compass: not a set of commands, but a framework for reflection.

Smith says: *Ask what a reasonable observer would say of your actions.* Mises says: *Remember that your actions express values, trade-offs, and goals.*

Put together, they're telling you something liberating: You don't need to be perfect. You need to be aware. You don't need to save the world. But you are always participating in it, whether you realize it or not.

Every time you choose to listen instead of react, to trade instead of take, to pause instead of punish - you strengthen the fabric of civilization. Not through grand gestures, but through what Smith called *propriety*: the quiet practice of doing what fits, what is right, in each moment.

From Mirror to Marketplace

Later chapters will explore what happens when these internal forces - sympathy, judgment, rational choice - scale up into systems: markets, governments, institutions. But I wanted to begin here, in the heart, where all those systems originate.

Because a market, stripped of its moral actors, is just numbers.

A law, without empathy behind it, is just force.

And a society that forgets to *imagine* each other's lives will soon find itself unable to live together at all.

Smith saw this in the 1700s. Mises sharpened it in the 1900s. And now, in a time of deep division and shallow discourse, we need to recover it in the 21st century.

Not as nostalgia.

But as necessity.

Chapter 2: Why Self-Interest Isn't Selfish

The Moral Heart of a Misunderstood Idea

When I hear the phrase *"self-interest,"* I picture the usual suspects: Wall Street suits, cutthroat tycoons, reality TV moguls with golden nameplates on private jets. For decades, the term has been flattened, distorted, and tossed around like a synonym for greed. But the truth - taught by Adam Smith and radically clarified by Ludwig von Mises - is almost the opposite.

Self-interest, properly understood, is not the villain of a good society. It's the foundation.

It's the reason you get out of bed. The reason you brush your teeth, care for your children, pay your bills, and build a better life. It is not about selfishness - it is about *agency*. The ability to make choices in pursuit of what matters to you. And when structured wisely, self-interest becomes the invisible glue of civilization.

Let me explain.

The Myth of the Greedy Individual

We've inherited a cartoon version of capitalism. You know the one: ruthless executives, hoarding wealth, exploiting workers, dodging taxes. And yes - bad actors exist. But to assume that capitalism *requires* selfishness is like saying democracy requires demagogues. It confuses *possibility* with *principle*.

Adam Smith never said greed was good. In fact, he was deeply skeptical of those who chased wealth for its own sake. What he did say - most famously in *The Wealth of Nations* - was this:

"It is not from the benevolence of the butcher, the brewer, or the baker that we expect our dinner, but from their regard to their own interest."

At first glance, this might sound cold. But look closer. Smith isn't mocking morality. He's describing a miracle: when systems are structured correctly, your effort to help yourself *can* become an act of helping others.

Let's take a simple example.

The Pizza Shop on the Corner

Imagine a neighborhood pizza shop. The owner, Maria, wants to make a living. That's her self-interest. So she opens a small business, hires workers, and starts serving the best crust in town.

To succeed, Maria must *think about others*. She needs to understand her customers' tastes, keep her prices fair, pay her team, manage her supply chain. If she cuts corners or treats people poorly, her reputation suffers, and so does her bottom line.

This is self-interest - yes. But it's *cooperative* self-interest. It is shaped by feedback, competition, accountability. And it produces something real: food, jobs, satisfaction. The customers get dinner, the employees get wages, and Maria gets a chance at prosperity.

Everyone is better off - not *because* Maria is an altruist, but because the system turns her effort into mutual gain.

That's the Smithian vision. And it's far more moral than it gets credit for.

Mises: The Science of Choosing

Ludwig von Mises took Smith's insight and built a precise logical structure around it. In *Human Action*, he argued that all purposeful behavior is driven by *the removal of felt uneasiness*. In plain terms: we act to make our lives better. Every decision - whether economic, social, or moral - is a trade-off between what is and what could be.

But here's where Mises departs from caricature: he insisted that this principle is *universal*. Not just billionaires or bankers - but artists, parents, monks, teachers. Choosing to donate to charity is a self-interested act. So is moving to a safer neighborhood. So is volunteering at a soup kitchen.

Because in each case, the actor is pursuing a preferred state of affairs. A sense of peace. A vision of rightness.

Does that mean morality is an illusion?

Not at all. It means morality lives inside our preferences - and our preferences can be deeply noble.

The Social Beauty of Self-Interest

Let's go back to Maria for a second. Imagine she starts noticing food insecurity in her neighborhood. Some kids show up hungry. Instead of just running a business, she starts a pay-it-forward program. Customers can donate to fund slices for those in need.

Is Maria still acting in her self-interest?

Yes. But not in a cynical way. Her "felt uneasiness" isn't about money - it's about justice. About dignity. Her moral impulse is real - and her action is still a form of choosing, just like any economic transaction.

The brilliance of Smith and Mises is that they recognized this continuum: that moral and market behavior are not opposites, but expressions of the same human faculty - *the ability to choose purposefully.*

But What About the Ruthless?

A fair question. What about those who exploit others? What about Ponzi schemes, environmental destruction, predatory lending?

Here's where the structure of systems matters. Markets don't automatically reward virtue. They reward perceived value. And without rules, transparency, and culture, perceived value can be manipulated.

Smith knew this. That's why he supported certain roles for government: preventing fraud, enforcing contracts, and protecting the vulnerable. Mises knew it too - he warned that monopolies and cronyism distort true market signals.

So no, we should not worship markets blindly. But we must not blame *self-interest* for the sins of *bad incentives.*

A sharp knife can heal or harm. The problem isn't the blade. It's how it's used.

The Everyday Ethics of Choice

Let's bring this back to you.

Every day, you make hundreds of decisions shaped by self-interest: what to eat, where to work, who to help, how to vote. Some choices are small. Others are defining. But none are morally neutral. Even mundane acts - tipping a barista, switching jobs, mentoring a coworker - ripple outward.

When your self-interest includes fairness, honesty, excellence, and empathy, you don't just succeed - you build.

That's the magic of a society built on voluntary exchange. It doesn't assume you're a saint. It doesn't require you to be a martyr. It simply says: *When free people pursue good things in good ways, good things can multiply.*

Self-Interest in Crisis

Let's test this idea in a harder place.

Think of the early days of the COVID-19 pandemic. Panic buying. Stockpiling. Lockdowns. Fear was rampant - and self-interest often looked ugly.

But look again.

Why did so many people stay home, mask up, or deliver groceries to neighbors? Not because of mandates alone. But because they *chose* to. They felt uneasiness - and resolved it with compassion. They didn't want others to suffer. That was their preference. That was their purpose.

Even in crisis, self-interest did not vanish. It transformed.

That transformation - when morality fuses with motivation - is what Smith and Mises help us understand.

The Call to Reclaim Self-Interest

We need to rescue this idea from its reputation.

We need to teach children that self-interest is not selfishness, but stewardship. That markets are not zero-sum games, but platforms for cooperation. That morality is not a sermon, but a sequence of choices - and each choice builds or breaks the world.

Self-interest is the seed of every great endeavor. It is what built bridges, cured diseases, composed symphonies, and launched satellites. It is also what holds hands, comforts friends, and writes books like this one.

So don't be ashamed of wanting a better life. But be conscious of what "better" means - and how your choices touch others.

That is the moral weight of freedom.

That is the heart of the human project.

And that is where we go next.

Chapter 3: Order Without a Master

The Power of Spontaneous Systems

We're conditioned to trust things that look planned. A well-organized calendar. A master blueprint. A five-year strategy. There's something comforting in believing that order requires orchestration - like the invisible baton of a maestro guiding an orchestra. But what if I told you that some of the most powerful, stable, and beautiful systems in human history were built without anyone planning them at all?

What if *order* can arise not from command, but from cooperation?

That's the heart of the next insight that Adam Smith and Ludwig von Mises give us: the world works *not* because someone controls it, but because people pursue their own ends, guided by information, incentives, and mutual adjustment. That phenomenon is called **spontaneous order** - and it's nothing short of a civilizational superpower.

Let's walk into it.

The Market: A Symphony Without a Conductor

Picture your local supermarket.

Walk down the bread aisle and consider: the flour was milled in one state, the yeast cultured in another, the packaging manufactured across the country. Maybe the machinery came from Germany, the software from India, the truck fleet from Detroit. Somehow, without any central planner coordinating all of it, a fresh loaf of bread appears on the shelf - on time, every morning - for a price you can afford.

How?

Each participant in that process - farmer, trucker, accountant, graphic designer - is acting in their own self-interest. They don't know you. They don't need to. What they *do* know is that participating in this chain, reliably and efficiently, benefits them.

That is the invisible order Smith spoke of in *The Wealth of Nations.*

And it's not magic.

It's the emergent result of *millions* of decentralized decisions responding to price signals, feedback loops, trust mechanisms, and reputational incentives. No president or think tank could ever replicate it.

In Smith's words:

"By pursuing his own interest, [a person] frequently promotes that of the society more effectually than when he really intends to promote it."

Mises and the Price Signal

If Smith marveled at spontaneous order, Mises *explained* it.

In *Human Action*, Mises revealed how prices are not just numbers on tags - they are **packets of information**. They tell us what is scarce and what is abundant, what people want and what they're willing to give up to get it.

Imagine a storm destroys half the orange crop in Florida. Orange juice prices rise. To a consumer, that might be annoying. But to a farmer in California or Mexico, it's a *signal* - produce more oranges. Ship them here. Serve a need. Make a profit.

All without a single meeting.

That's the brilliance of decentralized systems. Prices coordinate behavior more efficiently than any bureaucrat ever could. They are the language of spontaneous cooperation.

Spontaneous Systems in Everyday Life

Markets aren't the only example. In fact, spontaneous order is *everywhere*.

- **Language** evolved through millions of conversations, not government commissions.

- **Etiquette** - the way we queue in lines, say "thank you," or shake hands - emerged through repeated social trial and error.

- **The Internet** grew not from a single plan, but from collaborative protocols and voluntary participation.

- Even **Wikipedia**, chaotic as it seems, creates vast stores of human knowledge with no central editor-in-chief.

We assume order requires control. But often, control *kills* flexibility. It stifles innovation. It replaces voluntary adjustment with rigid command.

And here's the irony: the more control you try to impose, the more chaos you often create.

When Planning Goes Wrong

Let's consider a historical contrast.

In the mid-20th century, two countries tried to feed their people: the United States and the Soviet Union. The U.S. relied largely on decentralized farming and market incentives. The USSR imposed quotas, price controls, and central plans.

Guess who faced repeated famines?

The Soviet Union, despite having some of the richest farmland on earth, couldn't match the responsiveness of voluntary cooperation. Farmers lied about yields to meet quotas. Grain spoiled because transport schedules didn't adapt. Incentives collapsed. Corruption soared.

This isn't just a critique of communism. It's a lesson about human systems: **you can't plan complexity from the top down.** You need feedback. You need freedom.

Mises predicted this with chilling precision.

The Knowledge Problem

One of the most powerful ideas to come out of the Austrian tradition - first hinted at by Smith, crystallized by Mises, and sharpened by Friedrich Hayek - is the **knowledge problem**.

It goes like this:

No central planner can ever possess all the knowledge required to make rational economic decisions. That knowledge is dispersed across millions of minds, embedded in local contexts, preferences, constraints, and expectations.

You know the needs of your household better than any committee does.

A carpenter knows which tool is dull. A barista knows which item customers keep asking for. A nurse knows when a treatment is working or not. That is *tacit knowledge* - the kind of insight that can't be captured in spreadsheets or flowcharts.

Markets - when free - *harness* that knowledge. Planning *ignores* it.

The Fragility of Fragile Systems

You might ask: but don't we need planners for the big stuff? Healthcare, climate change, education?

Fair question. And it deserves a nuanced answer.

Spontaneous systems work best when they are allowed to *adapt*. But they can't do that when paralyzed by rigid central control. The goal should not be *no planning*, but *distributed planning* - local solutions, flexible feedback, optionality.

When the COVID pandemic struck, governments raced to centralize responses. Some worked. Many didn't. The most resilient models weren't those with strict top-down rules, but those that allowed local communities, businesses, and hospitals to adapt quickly.

The same principle applies to education, housing, and energy. The further the decision-making moves from the people directly affected, the more brittle the result.

Trusting the Process

This isn't just theory. It's a call to humility.

Spontaneous order requires us to trust something deeper than command: *the process of voluntary cooperation*. That trust doesn't come easily. It feels safer to believe in experts, programs, committees. But in reality, true experts thrive in systems where failure is allowed - and corrected - not buried beneath political pride.

When a pizza place messes up your order, you leave a bad review. When a government program fails, it asks for more funding.

One has feedback. The other has inertia.

Building with the Grain

Here's what I've come to believe: good societies don't try to impose order from above. They build *with the grain* of human nature. They create spaces where self-interest aligns with service. Where people are free to experiment, collaborate, and respond to changing needs.

That's what a free market is - not a jungle of greed, but a jungle gym of cooperation. Messy, yes. But alive. Creative. Resilient.

Smith saw this in the rise of commerce and civil society. Mises saw it in the collapse of central planning. And we see it every day - whenever people solve problems together without being told to.

You can see it in the sharing of a recipe. In the open-source software that runs your phone. In the community garden down the street.

That's order. Real order.

And no one is in charge of it.

What This Means for You

If you're a policymaker, this means resisting the temptation to micromanage what people can often solve themselves.

If you're an entrepreneur, this means trusting that markets will reward solutions - not slogans.

If you're a citizen, this means supporting systems that adapt, not systems that ossify.

And for all of us, it means recognizing the dignity of bottom-up effort. The miracle of coordination. The silent wisdom of freedom.

Spontaneous order isn't chaotic. It's elegant.

It's not leaderless. It's leaderful.

It's not perfect. But it is powerful.

And in the next chapter, we'll explore the most powerful moral resource it depends on - **trust**.

Chapter 4: Trust, Reputation, and the Hidden Currency of Civilization

Why Moral Capital Holds the Market Together

Imagine this: you're buying something from an online seller you've never met. You input your credit card, click "purchase," and wait - without ever considering whether the seller will send the item, whether the bank will process the transaction, or whether your package will show up at your door. You assume it will.

That assumption - that *strangers* will do what they say - is nothing short of a miracle.

And yet, we rarely marvel at it.

Behind every swipe, click, handshake, and promise in our daily lives lies a **hidden currency** - one more foundational than dollars or digital coins. It's called **trust**.

This chapter explores why trust is the true capital of a free society, how *reputation* acts as its storehouse, and why the moral behaviors Adam Smith and Ludwig von Mises described are not luxuries - they're the preconditions for prosperity.

The Thin Line Between Commerce and Chaos

Let's zoom out.

In a market society, we rely on millions of people we'll never meet: bakers, drivers, software developers, engineers, maintenance workers, nurses, bankers. The complexity of modern life is staggering. And yet - despite all the moving parts - it works.

Most of the time.

How?

Because we've embedded expectations into our daily interactions: that people will tell the truth, honor contracts, and deliver what they promised. These expectations are not enforced by physical force. They're enforced by something even more powerful: **social consequence**.

This is where Smith's early work on morality ties seamlessly into economics.

In *The Theory of Moral Sentiments*, he wrote:

"Man naturally desires, not only to be loved, but to be lovely."

That is, we want not just affection but *approval* - to be seen as good, competent, respectable. This desire fuels behavior. It restrains cruelty. It incentivizes generosity. It anchors the norms of a functioning society.

In a marketplace, this principle becomes economic gravity.

Reputation: The Interest-Bearing Account of Morality

Think of reputation like a personal credit score - except it tracks your moral reliability instead of your financial one.

You build it slowly, through honesty, reliability, kindness, excellence. And you can lose it quickly - with one act of fraud, deceit, or betrayal. Once lost, rebuilding it is brutally hard.

For a business, reputation *is* capital. A trusted brand can charge more, attract better talent, weather economic storms. A shady brand collapses in crisis.

For individuals, reputation determines opportunity. It influences hiring, promotion, lending, even friendship. In short: the more people believe you will do what is right when no one is watching, the more value you bring - not just morally, but practically.

This is why, in a free society, **virtue pays**.

Mises and the Rational Trust Builder

Mises, ever the clinical analyst, framed human behavior in terms of purposeful action. And he would argue that building trust is one of the most *rational* things an actor can do - because the benefits compound.

If you're a baker in a small town, you could cut corners to save money. Use cheaper flour. Reuse day-old dough. The customer might not notice - at first.

But over time, something erodes.

The flavor. The experience. The loyalty.

Eventually, the cost of that lost trust outweighs the short-term savings. So you stop cutting corners. Not because you've read philosophy books, but because *you've calculated the value of trust.*

This is the quiet genius of the market system when it's functioning well: it rewards those who think long-term about reputation, service, and consistency. And those who abuse trust find themselves priced out - sooner or later.

The Moral Infrastructure of Everyday Life

Let me show you where this gets practical.

1. Online Commerce

Platforms like Airbnb, Uber, and eBay don't operate because users love each other. They operate because **reputation is transparent**. One bad review dents your score. A pattern of misconduct gets you kicked off the platform.

These are spontaneous systems, built on the skeleton of trust. They work because everyone knows *everyone else is watching*.

2. Small Towns and Neighborhoods

In tight-knit communities, trust is even more direct. Gossip may seem trivial - but it's also a social enforcement mechanism. It rewards helpfulness and punishes betrayal. Neighbors lend tools, look after kids, share meals - not because of law, but because of **reciprocal trust**.

This is why moral capital - the trust built over time - is more valuable than regulation. You can't legislate friendship. You can't mandate goodwill.

You can only build it.

The Cost of Corruption

Now let's look at what happens when trust breaks down.

In countries with high corruption, everything slows down. Every transaction requires bribes, paperwork, guarantees. Legal systems can't be trusted. Officials can be bought. Contracts mean little.

Economists call this a *"trust tax."* And it's massive.

If people don't trust each other, they can't specialize. If they can't specialize, they can't trade efficiently. If they can't trade, they can't grow. Economic output stalls. Innovation dies. And worst of all, the moral tone of society declines: everyone begins to assume the worst in others.

In such environments, even the good become cynical. Integrity becomes risky. That is a tragic inversion of the Smithian vision.

The Modern Reputation Economy

We now live in what some call the *"reputation economy."* From Yelp stars to LinkedIn endorsements, every click becomes a kind of moral feedback. And while this can be toxic in excess - feeding mob behavior and cancel culture - it also democratizes accountability.

Small businesses can thrive with stellar reviews. Individuals can signal credibility without credentials. Artists can find audiences without agents.

But none of that works without trust.

And trust can't exist without repeated moral action.

So even in the age of AI and digital everything, the ancient truths Smith wrote about still apply: *We want to be respected. We care what others think. And those desires shape our decisions.*

Institutions and the Trust Dividend

Let's widen the lens again.

Countries with high trust enjoy what I call the **"trust dividend."** They need fewer audits, fewer police, fewer inspectors. People pay taxes more willingly.

Businesses follow laws more voluntarily. The result? Lower costs, faster systems, more innovation.

Compare this to low-trust societies, where even basic governance is a struggle. Everything requires enforcement. That creates bottlenecks, inefficiencies, and conflict.

Trust is a lubricant. Without it, even well-designed machines grind to a halt.

So when people say "capitalism doesn't work," they often mean *trustless capitalism doesn't work*. And they're right.

Markets without morals are like cars without oil - they overheat, stall, and sometimes explode.

Rebuilding Trust in a Distracted World

We live in an age of fractured attention and eroding institutions. Many people no longer trust the media, government, or even their neighbors. Polarization has turned disagreement into distrust, and distrust into disgust.

Can we reverse this?

Yes - but not with slogans.

We need *practice*.

We need more micro-interactions where people experience fairness, respect, and follow-through. That's how trust is rebuilt - not in grand gestures, but in daily decisions. In being five minutes early. In calling when you say you will. In delivering the pizza hot.

These small acts are not trivial. They are the foundations of civilizational scale.

Your Moral Credit Score

So here's my challenge to you:

Treat trust like a bank account.

Every promise kept is a deposit. Every lie is a withdrawal. Every extra mile walked for someone else is a compounded investment.

And reputation? That's your balance sheet. Not flashy, not loud - but visible to those who matter.

The truth is, we can't download character. We can't outsource virtue. In a free society, the only way we keep moving forward is by **believing that others will do the right thing even when they don't have to.**

That belief isn't naïve.

It's necessary.

It's the backbone of every handshake, every transaction, every long-term plan.

And in the next chapter, we'll explore how this invisible currency limits the power of visible law - and why *character* is more important than any regulation could ever be.

Chapter 5: The Limits of Law and the Rise of Character

Why Virtue Outperforms Regulation in a Free Society

A law can make you stop at a red light. It can punish theft, require licenses, or cap interest rates. But no law - no matter how clever or comprehensive - can *make* you kind, honest, generous, or courageous.

That's not what laws do.

And that's exactly why Adam Smith and Ludwig von Mises understood something our modern world often forgets: **a society cannot be held together by law alone.**

Laws are guardrails, not engines. They prevent disaster, but they don't inspire excellence. They keep the worst instincts in check, but they don't nurture the best in us. For that, we need something deeper than statutes. We need *character*.

This chapter is about the moral muscle a free society depends on - and why, without it, even the best policies collapse into dysfunction.

Why We Can't Regulate Our Way to Goodness

Let's start with a provocative truth:

Every law is a confession of failure.

We pass laws when trust has been broken. When someone has lied, cheated, polluted, or defrauded. We legislate in reaction. And that's not wrong. Laws are necessary. They protect rights, resolve conflicts, and keep power in check. But laws are blunt tools. They can't read hearts. They can't adapt on the fly. They can't sense nuance or kindness or grace.

Consider customer service.

You could write a hundred rules about politeness - what tone to use, how fast to reply, what words are forbidden. But the best service doesn't come from compliance. It comes from *care*. From a person choosing to see another person and say: *I want to make this better.*

That's character in action. And you can't legislate that.

Smith and the Moral Imagination

Adam Smith knew this intimately. In *The Theory of Moral Sentiments*, he described the birth of moral awareness not in courts or parliaments, but in the human heart. He understood that the most important judge is not the one in robes - it's the **"impartial spectator"** within us.

When you feel the sting of guilt or the lift of pride, that's not law at work. That's conscience.

And here's the kicker: **the freer a society is, the more it depends on internal judgment.**

In a tyranny, morality doesn't matter - obedience does. But in a free society, where people choose their actions, speak their minds, start businesses, and vote leaders into power, the internal compass is everything.

Without it, freedom becomes chaos. Or worse, corruption.

Mises and the Limits of Coercion

Mises took a harder-edged view. In *Human Action*, he made it clear: laws that go beyond protecting life, liberty, and property tend to backfire. Why? Because human action is purposeful. If you force someone to act against their interests, they will either resist, circumvent, or distort the system to survive.

The more laws you create to "fix" morality, the more bureaucracy you build. And the more bureaucracy you build, the less responsive, honest, and human your society becomes.

Think about tax codes.

You want people to pay their fair share? Sure. But the more complex the system, the more loopholes, lawyers, lobbyists. People follow the letter and ignore the spirit. The system becomes a game. Trust erodes.

What you needed wasn't just more rules - you needed more **integrity**.

Character: The Low-Tech, High-Impact Solution

Here's a radical idea in a world obsessed with systems and hacks:

The greatest upgrade to any society is people choosing to be better than they are required to be.

This shows up in every corner of life:

- A manager who tells the truth even when the numbers are bad.

- A contractor who finishes the job properly even when no one's watching.

- A teenager who returns a lost wallet instead of keeping the cash.

- A customer who forgives a mistake and shows grace.

These moments don't just feel good - they *create trust*. They model behavior. They teach others that moral excellence isn't rare - it's real.

And when enough people act this way, you need fewer cops. Fewer lawyers. Fewer locks.

Character scales better than control.

The Problem with Policy-Centric Thinking

Modern politics suffers from a peculiar disease: the belief that **every problem must have a policy solution.**

Low productivity? Write a program. Broken families? Expand services. Loneliness? Fund community centers.

Now, none of these responses are wrong on their face. But they share a common flaw: they assume that *what people lack is structure*, not spirit.

But what if what's missing is *responsibility*?

What if we have created systems so focused on protecting people from consequences that we've eroded the very capacity for character to develop?

Smith believed in moral development through relationships, feedback, admiration, and shame. Mises believed in action shaped by incentives and purpose. Both would argue that **no subsidy, regulation, or mandate can substitute for a person saying, "I will do the right thing - even when I don't have to."**

Character in Institutions

This isn't just about individuals. Institutions have character too.

Think of a school that passes students regardless of effort. A company that sells defective products. A government that makes promises it can't keep. These are not systems failing to function - they are systems functioning *without integrity.*

And what happens?

People stop believing.

They opt out. Or worse, they mimic the dysfunction. Corruption spreads not because people are evil - but because **they see no reward for goodness.**

So the real challenge is cultural, not technical.

We must rebuild the moral tone of institutions. Reward honesty. Celebrate long-term thinking. Restore the link between virtue and viability.

That's not a job for algorithms.

That's a job for leaders with character.

A Modern Parable

Let me give you a story.

A mid-sized construction company once ran into a dilemma. A client had paid for a new office build, but after an unexpected storm, the site was damaged. The contract had a clause: "Acts of God" released the company from liability.

Legally, they could walk away.

But the owner said, "If I were the client, I'd want the job finished."

So he did.

At a loss. Quietly. No press release.

Years later, that same client recommended him to multiple partners. The business grew. Not because of marketing. But because of **moral memory**.

That's the ROI of character.

And it outperforms any contract.

What This Means for Us

So where do we go from here?

1. **Raise the bar for yourself.** Don't do the minimum. Build your own moral infrastructure.

2. **Reward character in others.** Support businesses, leaders, and neighbors who act with integrity.

3. **Design systems that encourage virtue.** Focus less on control, more on trust and feedback.

4. **Teach moral imagination.** Help children and peers *see* from others' perspectives - because that's how the impartial spectator grows.

Above all, stop waiting for laws to save us.

Laws restrain. But they don't inspire.

Character does.

The Free Society Needs the Moral One

Adam Smith believed freedom could only thrive if tethered to virtue.

Mises believed the same - though from a different lens. He saw that without moral judgment, human action can become predatory, parasitic, or nihilistic.

So if we want a world of dignity, prosperity, and peace, we must raise a generation of people who choose excellence not out of fear, but out of *conviction*.

We must build systems that amplify - not replace - character.

Because in the end, it is not the rulebook that saves us.

It is the soul.

PART II:

CHOICE, VALUE, AND HUMAN ACTION

Chapter 6: The Individual is the Architect

Mises and the Meaning of Human Action

Close your eyes for a moment.

Picture a city skyline - towering buildings, flickering windows, people streaming through subways, buying coffee, writing code, sweeping sidewalks, protesting, praying, dreaming. Every movement, every transaction, every heartbeat of that city - what holds it together?

Not a central command. Not an omniscient planner.

It's held together by **choice**.

Each of those individuals - whether aware of it or not - is engaged in what Ludwig von Mises called the defining feature of our species: **purposeful behavior.** Not instinct. Not reaction. But *intentional action* aimed at achieving something better than the current state of things.

That's human action. And it's the most radical, liberating, and empowering concept in all of economic philosophy.

In this chapter, we'll uncover Mises' view of the individual not just as a participant in society - but as its architect. Not a pawn, but a planner. Not a cog in a machine, but the machine's designer.

Because once we understand what human action really means, the rest of this book - and the rest of life - snaps into clarity.

Human Action: A Simple but Powerful Idea

Mises' central thesis in his magnum opus *Human Action* is deceptively simple:

All human behavior is purposeful.

We act when we are dissatisfied with our current state and envision a more satisfactory one. We apply means to achieve ends. We make decisions under uncertainty. Every choice, however small, reflects a goal, an evaluation of options, and a belief in a better outcome.

Sounds basic?

It is. But the implications are seismic.

If all human behavior is purposeful, then:

- People are not passive.
- Value is subjective.
- Trade is mutual improvement.
- Progress is directional, not random.
- Systems must serve the chooser - not the other way around.

This means that *you*, reader, are not a statistic. You're not a "consumer segment" or "labor unit" or "voter bloc." You are a conscious actor in the world - deciding, shaping, pursuing, adapting.

And the world responds to you.

Means, Ends, and Choice Under Scarcity

Let's break down the building blocks of Misesian action:

1. Ends: These are your goals - anything you wish to achieve, whether noble or trivial. To get fit. To feed your family. To win an argument. To feel loved.

2. Means: These are the tools, strategies, or resources you use to pursue your ends. A gym membership. A dinner recipe. A tweet. A hug.

3. Choice: This is the moment of trade-off. You can't have everything. Time, money, energy - these are all scarce. So you prioritize. You choose what's more important *to you*, right now.

This is economics in its purest form - not GDP charts or stock prices, but **everyday decision-making under constraint**.

When your alarm goes off and you hit snooze, you're acting. When you donate to charity, you're acting. When you study late instead of going out, you're acting.

Each choice reveals your values - not in theory, but in practice.

This is what makes Mises' view so *human*. It doesn't reduce us to numbers. It elevates us as agents of our own destiny.

Subjective Value: Why Price Tags Are Personal

One of the most powerful implications of human action is the concept of **subjective value**.

There's no universal price for anything - not for coffee, not for art, not even for time. Value is *personal*. What something is worth to you depends on your preferences, your context, your goals.

That's why someone might pay $8 for a latte while another brews theirs at home for 50 cents. Same drink. Different value. Different ends.

Markets, then, aren't about finding "true" prices. They're about **discovering what people care about - and how much they care.**

This is not chaos. It's coordination.

And it only works if people are free to act on their values.

Which leads us to the next insight.

The Power of Voluntary Exchange

When two people engage in trade - whether it's money for goods, time for attention, or effort for affection - they do so because **each expects to be better off.**

That's not zero-sum. It's positive-sum.

Trade is not theft. It's transformation.

This is why markets, when free and fair, are moral systems. They allow individuals to solve problems, discover value, and improve their lives - not by force, but by **mutual agreement**.

Smith hinted at this with his "butcher, brewer, baker" example.

Mises built the logic tower: if all human action is aimed at improvement, and trade allows both parties to improve, then trade is not exploitation - it's the **expression of human dignity**.

The freedom to choose is the freedom to grow.

Institutions Built on Choice

Let's bring this idea into real life.

1. Entrepreneurship

A startup founder sees unmet needs and launches a product. That's not charity - it's action. She invests time, risk, and capital to remove uneasiness - hers and others'. Every decision she makes - from hiring to pricing - is a purposeful strategy. If she misjudges? The market tells her. If she succeeds? Everyone wins.

2. Education

A student doesn't absorb knowledge passively. He chooses to learn, to focus, to apply. Good teachers don't "fill brains" - they design incentives, spark curiosity, and honor the agency of their students.

3. Politics

Voting is human action, too. It's a statement about values, trade-offs, and imagined futures. Good political systems recognize this and respect the chooser. Bad ones treat people as numbers to be manipulated.

Wherever systems empower action, people flourish. Wherever they suppress it, people stagnate.

The Tragedy of Coerced Action

So what happens when action is replaced by coercion?

What happens when people no longer choose their ends, but have them assigned?

Mises warned us: such systems breed resentment, inefficiency, and decay.

- A centrally planned economy assumes the planner knows your ends better than you.

- A bureaucratic state assumes it must limit your options to "guide" you.

- A culture of dependency assumes you can't act purposefully, so others must act for you.

These systems are not just wrong economically - they are wrong **morally**. They deny human beings the very thing that makes them human: the right - and responsibility - to choose.

This doesn't mean we abandon safety nets or social support. It means we design them to **empower**, not infantilize.

It means we treat the poor, the sick, the struggling not as passive recipients - but as actors capable of making better lives when given tools, not chains.

Responsibility: The Shadow Side of Freedom

Here's where things get hard.

If you are the architect of your life, then your successes - and failures - are yours.

That's the burden of liberty.

But it's also the gift.

Responsibility is not a punishment. It is the soil from which growth emerges. When we deny it, we create dependence. When we embrace it, we create resilience.

This is why Mises' worldview is so empowering - and so demanding.

It refuses to let you blame "the system," "the elite," or "bad luck" forever. It asks: *What are you doing with what you have? What uneasiness are you removing? What value are you creating?*

And if you're not happy with your answers - it says, *You can choose again.*

The Hidden Beauty of Ordinary Action

Let's not romanticize this.

Most human action is not dramatic. It's not starting companies or writing manifestos. It's making lunch. Answering emails. Putting kids to bed.

But even these acts - mundane as they seem - carry meaning.

Each one expresses values. Each one shapes your world. Each one is part of the great mosaic of a free society - where millions of people pursue countless ends, solve each other's problems, and build something no central planner ever could.

It's not perfect. It's messy. But it's *alive.*

And it starts with one truth: **you are not a victim of the world. You are its co-creator.**

Why This Changes Everything

If you accept the Misesian view - that every person is a purposeful actor - then everything else changes:

- **Education** becomes about cultivating decision-makers.

- **Economics** becomes the study of choices, not just numbers.

- **Politics** becomes about protecting the space to choose.

- **Morality** becomes personal and situational - not because ethics are relative, but because the good life is always chosen, never imposed.

You are not a statistic.

You are not defined by your group, your race, your gender, or your class.

You are an agent.

And the world is shaped, every day, by people like you making decisions - one purposeful action at a time.

Chapter 7: The Seen, the Unseen, and the Intentionally Ignored

How Hidden Costs and Forgotten Consequences Shape Our World

In the middle of the 19th century, a French economist named **Frédéric Bastiat** wrote a simple, almost humorous essay called *That Which is Seen, and That Which is Not Seen*. In it, he tells the story of a shopkeeper whose son breaks a window. Onlookers try to console the man by saying, "At least this will be good for the glazier - it's economic activity!"

But Bastiat sees through the fallacy. Yes, the glazier earns six francs. But what about what is *not* seen - the tailor who won't get paid now, the suit that won't be made, the value that vanishes because resources had to be redirected to fix something broken?

What Bastiat revealed is something both **Adam Smith** and **Ludwig von Mises** understood deeply:

Every human action has both immediate and downstream consequences. Some are visible. Most are not. And when we ignore the unseen, we make dangerous decisions.

This idea - so simple in theory - explains why entire civilizations rise or fall. It explains bad policies, broken systems, ballooning debt, and unintended social crises. And it gives us a crucial tool for navigating the modern world: *economic imagination.*

Let's sharpen that tool now.

The Temptation of the Tangible

Modern society is obsessed with the visible: results you can measure, show, post, brag about. Metrics, dashboards, news headlines.

But reality is richer than a spreadsheet. Much of what truly matters lies beneath the surface.

Take a new government jobs program. Politicians love ribbon-cuttings and press releases. "We created 10,000 jobs!" they boast.

But what's unseen?

- Where did the money come from?

- Which private sector jobs never materialized because taxes went up?

- What innovations were delayed because entrepreneurs couldn't hire?

- What unintended behavior was incentivized?

These are not rhetorical questions. They're the hidden half of every policy.

And if we don't ask them - if we focus only on what is seen - we risk creating **mirages of prosperity that mask real decline**.

Mises and the Law of Unintended Consequences

Ludwig von Mises took Bastiat's idea and gave it mathematical rigor. He warned again and again: **intervening in complex systems without understanding second- and third-order effects will almost always backfire.**

Here's a modern example: rent control.

On paper, it sounds noble. Cap rents so people can afford to live in cities.

But Mises would ask: What happens next?

- Landlords defer maintenance.
- Builders avoid constructing new units.
- Black markets emerge for housing.
- Affordability declines in the long run.
- Quality of life deteriorates.

These are not hypotheticals. They've played out in New York, San Francisco, Berlin, Stockholm. Every time, the short-term "help" becomes long-term harm.

The lesson? **When the state sets prices, it blinds itself to information.** And when it blinds itself, it loses the ability to allocate resources well.

The cost isn't just financial. It's *human*.

The Myth of Stimulus

Let's consider another popular fallacy: that government spending during recessions is always helpful because "it gets money flowing."

Mises - and Bastiat - would raise eyebrows.

55

When the government spends, it must first **take**. That might mean taxation. Or it might mean printing money, which erodes purchasing power through inflation.

Either way, resources are **not created - they're redirected.**

The road is paved, yes. The bridge is built. But what didn't get built instead? What dreams didn't get funded? What investments were discouraged by the uncertainty?

These questions are *rarely* asked in public debate. Why?

Because the consequences are **diffuse**, **delayed**, and **difficult to trace.**

But they're no less real.

Personal Life: The Unseen in Our Daily Decisions

This principle doesn't only apply to governments and economists. It shapes *our lives*, too.

Imagine you choose to binge-watch a show instead of learning a new skill. The benefit is immediate and visible - relaxation, entertainment. But what's unseen?

- The book you didn't read.
- The confidence you didn't build.
- The career growth you postponed.

Or consider a parent who constantly rescues their child from natural consequences. The child may seem happy in the short term. But what's unseen?

- The resilience not built.
- The decision-making not learned.

- The maturity not developed.

This is not about guilt. It's about *awareness*. Mises taught us that all action involves trade-offs. Bastiat taught us to *look harder at what's missing*.

Together, they teach us to live with our eyes wider open.

Incentives, Perverse and Otherwise

When we ignore the unseen, we don't just waste resources - we warp **incentives.**

Let's say a city pays hospitals for every COVID-19 test administered. Great! More testing.

But what if some providers start inflating their numbers? What if time and attention shift away from treatment to paperwork? What if the incentive distorts priorities?

That's not fiction. That happened.

Or consider this: a government subsidizes corn. Farmers grow more. But now processed food companies have cheap inputs. So sugary snacks flood the market. Obesity rises. Healthcare costs explode.

None of this was the *intent*. But it was the *effect*.

And that's the lesson: **intentions don't matter. Outcomes do.**

Why Politicians Love the Seen

It's easy to bash government here, so let's ask: *why* do politicians love the visible?

Simple: **political survival is short-term.**

The ribbon-cutting happens today. The deficit ballooning happens after the next election. The inflation spike comes years later. By then, someone else takes the blame.

Mises saw this clearly. He warned that **politics tends to favor spectacle over substance**. It overweights current voters and underweights future generations.

Which is why economic policy, like parenting or investing, must be **rooted in principle - not popularity.**

What Smith Adds: The Moral Lens

Adam Smith enriches this conversation in a vital way: by reminding us that our **moral instincts** are also vulnerable to the seen/unseen trap.

We weep for visible suffering - and rightly so. But we often ignore **suffering caused by our attempts to alleviate suffering**.

We feed the hungry - but sometimes destroy local agriculture in the process.

We rescue addicts - but sometimes extend their pain by removing consequences.

Smith's impartial spectator - our internal moral judge - must be trained to see *beyond the immediate*. It must ask: "What are the effects of this, not just now - but later, and to others?"

Moral maturity means *being patient enough to see further*.

Cultivating Economic Imagination

What's the solution?

We need to **develop economic imagination** - the ability to think in systems, not snapshots. To ask:

- What's not obvious here?
- What else might this change?
- Who benefits - and who pays?
- What behavior is this encouraging?
- What ripple effects might this create?

This doesn't mean becoming paralyzed or cynical. It means becoming **curious**. Asking deeper questions. Slowing down our desire to "fix" things without understanding them.

Mises was fond of saying, "There is no such thing as a free lunch." Bastiat might add: "And sometimes, there's no such thing as a *cheap one*, either."

Personal Power: Choosing to See

Let me leave you with this.

You have more power than you think - not just to act, but to *perceive*. To train your mind to look beyond headlines, slogans, and surface-level solutions.

When you choose a job, support a candidate, give to charity, or speak up in a meeting - ask yourself: *What is seen? What is not seen? What am I choosing not to look at?*

Because often, the future is hidden in the second-order.

Wisdom begins when our eyes adjust.

Chapter 8: Scarcity and the Dance of Decision

Why Every Choice Is a Trade and Every Life a Series of Priorities

Time. Money. Energy. Attention. Goodwill. Space. Love.

All of these are limited.

And because they're limited, **we must choose.**

This is the simple truth economists mean when they say *scarcity*. But it's not just about physical goods or budget lines. Scarcity is the reason we can't be in two places at once, can't say yes to everything, and can't solve every problem all at once.

It's not a curse.

It's the *condition* of being human.

Scarcity is what makes our choices matter. If we had infinite resources, infinite time, and infinite stamina, we wouldn't need to prioritize, sacrifice, or evaluate. We wouldn't even need values - because nothing would cost anything.

But we *do* have limits.

And that's why economics, as Ludwig von Mises so often said, is ultimately not about money - it's about **human action under constraint**. It's about *decision-making* when not all desires can be fulfilled.

This chapter unpacks how scarcity forces us to choose, how value is revealed through what we *give up*, and how that truth - far from being depressing - is actually the heartbeat of progress, virtue, and civilization.

61

Scarcity Isn't a Problem - It's a Signal

Let's start by flipping the script.

When people hear the word "scarcity," they think of poverty, desperation, loss. But in economic terms, scarcity is not inherently bad. It's just real. It's the backdrop against which *every* meaningful decision is made.

If oxygen became scarce, we'd fight over it. But because it's abundant (in most cases), we don't think about it at all. No one opens an "oxygen shop" next to Starbucks.

Scarcity, therefore, creates **value.**

The more limited something is, and the more it satisfies our needs, the more we value it. And that value becomes visible in how we act - what we choose, what we sacrifice, what we pursue.

In other words:

Scarcity is the reason choice exists. And choice is the reason economics - and ethics - exist.

Opportunity Cost: What You Give Up

One of the most powerful tools for navigating scarcity is a concept economists call **opportunity cost**.

It means this: every time you say "yes" to something, you are saying "no" to something else.

You go out for dinner? That's money you're not saving.
You scroll social media? That's time you're not investing in your health or relationships.
You take one job? You're not taking another.

Every action has a cost - not just in dollars, but in what's *forgone*.

This isn't meant to make you anxious. It's meant to make you **mindful**.

Mises understood that people are constantly ranking preferences. Every action reveals what you *value more* in that moment. Not what you *should* value. Not what you *say* you value. But what you actually value when the trade-off is real.

And that's why economics, in his view, was not about systems - it was about *people*.

Marginal Utility: The More You Have, the Less It's Worth

Another crucial insight into scarcity comes from what's called **marginal utility**.

It sounds technical, but it's intuitive.

The first bite of pizza when you're hungry? Amazing.
The third slice? Still good.
The sixth slice? Regret.
The ninth slice? You may never eat pizza again.

That's marginal utility: **the value of an additional unit of something declines as you get more of it.**

This principle shapes everything from pricing to production. It's why diamonds are more expensive than water - even though water is essential. It's not the *total* usefulness that determines price - it's the *marginal* usefulness, the value of the *next* unit.

And that's also why income feels different across classes. An extra $500 means a lot more to a single parent than to a billionaire. Same dollars - radically different utility.

This matters deeply for both moral and policy reasons. Because we live in a world where resources must be allocated - and that means we need to understand how value changes depending on *who* holds it, and how they use it.

Scarcity Shapes Culture, Not Just Costs

Scarcity doesn't just influence individual decisions. It also shapes entire **cultures**.

- In subsistence economies, hospitality is rare - because food is scarce.

- In wealthy societies, time becomes the new scarcity - and people "buy" it with services: cleaners, food delivery, concierge apps.

- In war zones, trust is scarce - so alliances shift fast.

- In digital economies, **attention** becomes the ultimate scarcity - leading to algorithms that prey on dopamine and outrage.

What does this mean?

It means every culture, system, and norm is a reflection of *what people lack* - and what they're willing to trade to get more of it.

That's not cynical. It's clarifying.

Once you understand that people are navigating scarcity constantly, their behavior starts to make sense - even if it's frustrating or irrational on the surface.

They're not being stupid. They're responding to incentives you might not see.

Scarcity Creates Coordination - Through Markets

Here's where it gets beautiful.

When millions of people are facing different scarcities - money, time, knowledge, resources - they start trading with each other. Voluntarily. Repeatedly. Creatively.

That's a **market**.

You have too much firewood but not enough potatoes? Trade with your neighbor who has the opposite problem.

You have free time but no income? Sell your time for a wage.

You have money but no cooking skills? Pay for a meal.

Markets are not just about getting rich. They're about solving scarcity *together* - by allowing people to specialize, exchange, and serve each other's needs.

And the more open and honest the market, the more efficiently it allocates resources to those who value them most.

Mises saw this clearly. That's why he considered the market process not just economically sound, but morally elegant. It respects human dignity by allowing *each person* to define their own ends, and to act in pursuit of them.

Scarcity and the Morality of Limits

Let's now return to Smith.

Adam Smith believed that the moral self emerges not in abundance - but in limitation. We learn empathy, restraint, generosity, and perspective *because* we can't have everything. Because we must share, negotiate, compromise.

If everything were infinite, character would be irrelevant. Scarcity, then, is what makes **virtue visible**.

Consider parenting.

Every parent has a limited supply of time, energy, and money. How they spend it - on their kids, their career, their marriage, their health - reveals their values.

And every child, in turn, grows up learning to navigate scarcity too: waiting their turn, earning rewards, coping with disappointment. These are not failures of love - they are the **forge of maturity.**

A society that pretends scarcity doesn't exist - by printing money, removing accountability, or promising unlimited services - may feel compassionate in the short term. But it raises people who are unprepared for real life.

Compassion divorced from constraints becomes cruelty in disguise.

Scarcity in the Digital Age: The New Frontier

Here's a wrinkle.

In the digital world, many of the old scarcities vanish. We can copy music, books, code, and images infinitely. AI generates answers on demand. Streaming puts a universe of content at our fingertips.

But now, a *new* scarcity dominates: **attention**.

And once again, markets adapt.

Apps fight for your screen time. Notifications fight for your focus. Content creators compete for dopamine.

In this landscape, your *self-control* becomes the most valuable resource.

And that makes ethical clarity more important than ever.

Because in a world where everything is instantly accessible, the question becomes not "what can I have?" but *"what should I want?"*

Embracing Scarcity, Choosing Wisely

We cannot escape scarcity.

But we can **choose how we respond to it.**

- We can spend our energy chasing everything - or we can prioritize what matters.

- We can envy others' choices - or we can own our own.

- We can ignore opportunity costs - or we can count them honestly.

Mises gave us the economic tools. Smith gave us the moral compass.

Both understood: **to live freely and wisely is to choose purposefully - within limits - and to honor those limits as teachers, not enemies.**

Scarcity as the Ground of Gratitude

Let me leave you with this:

Scarcity, for all its harshness, is also the reason we *treasure* things.

We treasure a friend's time because it's not endless.
We treasure a sunset because it only lasts minutes.
We treasure childhood because it's fleeting.
We treasure character because it costs something to maintain.

When nothing costs anything, nothing means anything.

So don't curse your constraints.

Use them to become who you're meant to be.

Chapter 9: Why Central Planning Fails (Even with Supercomputers)

The Fatal Conceit of Control and the Triumph of Decentralized Intelligence

Imagine the brightest minds in the world, armed with the fastest computers, unlimited funding, and full political authority. Their goal? Design an economy that works for everyone. No poverty, no inequality, no chaos. Every factory, every farm, every family budget - perfectly accounted for and optimized from the top down.

Sounds utopian, right?

It's not.

It's a fantasy.

And not just because people are selfish or power corrupts - though those things matter. It's a fantasy because of something deeper, more inescapable, more profound:

No central planner - no matter how brilliant or benevolent - can ever access, process, or act upon the dispersed knowledge held by millions of individuals in real time.

This isn't ideology.

It's information theory.

And Ludwig von Mises was the first to see it clearly.

In this chapter, we'll examine why central planning fails - not just in Stalin's Russia or Mao's China, but *everywhere it's tried*. We'll explore why even advanced algorithms can't replicate the information-rich feedback loops of markets, and how both Adam Smith and Mises anticipated this modern problem long before computers entered the scene.

Because the problem isn't tech. It's *epistemic humility* - or the lack of it.

The Socialist Calculation Debate: Mises' Intellectual Battle

In 1920, Mises dropped a bombshell on the intellectual world.

At the height of enthusiasm for socialism, he published a paper arguing that **a socialist economy was *impossible*.**

Not inefficient. Not immoral. *Impossible.*

Why? Because socialism abolishes markets - and with them, *prices*. And without prices, you lose the ability to calculate economic value.

Let's unpack that.

In a market economy, prices emerge from voluntary exchange. They reflect real-time information about scarcity, preference, opportunity cost, and risk. They help producers decide what to make, how much, and for whom.

In a socialist economy, by contrast, the state owns the means of production. No buying or selling of capital goods. No prices. No decentralized exchange.

And without those signals?

Planners are flying blind.

They don't know whether to produce rubber boots or running shoes, wind turbines or washing machines. They don't know what people want. They don't know what materials are best used elsewhere. Every choice becomes a guess.

Mises called this the **calculation problem** - and no one could answer it.

Hayek's Enhancement: The Knowledge Problem

Mises' student, **Friedrich Hayek**, later deepened the argument with what became known as the **knowledge problem**:

Information is decentralized, tacit, and constantly changing - and no central authority can ever gather or update it fast enough to make efficient decisions.

Think of a local farmer who notices a pest outbreak. He switches crops. His customers adjust. The delivery route changes. His competitor lowers prices. All of this happens dynamically, without any formal reporting.

Now imagine trying to replicate that adjustment from a central office.

By the time the report is filed, the data is stale. By the time a decision is made, the market has moved. And by the time it's implemented, the damage is done.

This isn't just a logistical problem.

It's a **structural defect** in top-down planning.

But What About AI?

Let's jump to the 21st century.

Surely, you say, Mises and Hayek couldn't have foreseen *supercomputers*. Today, we have machine learning, real-time analytics, predictive algorithms. Couldn't those solve the knowledge problem?

It's tempting.

But the answer is still no.

Even the most powerful AI must be **fed data**. But the most crucial economic data - local knowledge, shifting preferences, personal risk tolerances, innovative ideas - *aren't in any database*. They live in minds, in relationships, in millions of micro-decisions made every day.

A computer can analyze patterns. But it cannot *discover value* without feedback from actual people, engaging in real exchange.

Mises anticipated this perfectly. He understood that **information is not just a product - it's a process.** And that process is only possible through *free interaction*.

That's why, even today, centrally planned economies underperform. They may use digital tools - but the underlying system still lacks *organic discovery*.

Historical Proof: When Planning Failed

Let's test this theory against reality.

1. Soviet Union

Command economy. Five-year plans. Industrial quotas. Result? Chronic shortages, mismatched production, food lines, and environmental disasters. Despite immense resources, the USSR could not feed its people reliably.

2. Mao's China

The Great Leap Forward centralized agricultural planning, banned private farming, and tried to industrialize by decree. The result? A famine that killed **tens of millions** - the deadliest in human history.

3. North Korea

Same language, same people, same geography as South Korea. But one chose central planning. The other embraced markets. Today, one is prosperous. The other is starving.

These aren't anomalies.

They're what happen **when planners replace people, and prices are replaced with plans.**

The False Comfort of Control

Why, then, does central planning still appeal to intellectuals, politicians, and activists?

Because **control feels comforting.** It offers the illusion of certainty. The promise of order. The belief that complexity can be tamed if only the right experts are in charge.

But this is what Hayek called **"the fatal conceit."**

It's not that planners are evil. It's that they are **overconfident in their knowledge and blind to what they can't know.**

And that blindness has real consequences. It leads to:

- Overbuilding and waste (ghost cities).
- Underproduction (food or fuel shortages).
- Rigid systems that can't adapt (pandemic supply chains).
- Corruption and favoritism (crony socialism).
- Apathy among citizens, who stop trying - because effort doesn't matter when outcomes are assigned.

When outcomes are disconnected from choices, initiative dies.

And with it, innovation.

The Moral Case Against Central Planning

We've talked economics. Now let's bring in **ethics**.

Adam Smith, for all his brilliance as an economist, was first a moral philosopher. He believed that human beings thrive when allowed to act according to their own values, judged by their peers, guided by their own conscience.

Central planning strips people of that agency.

It says: "We know better than you what your life should be like."

It replaces creativity with compliance. Choice with coercion. Aspiration with obedience.

Even when intentions are noble, the effect is infantilizing. It treats citizens as problems to be solved - not as participants to be trusted.

That's not just inefficient. It's *dehumanizing*.

Markets as Adaptive Intelligence

So if planning fails, what succeeds?

Not chaos.

But something much more powerful: **emergent order**.

Markets are not perfect. But they are **adaptive**. They respond. They correct. They evolve.

- When a product is bad, consumers walk away.
- When a service is excellent, it grows.
- When needs shift, supply chains reconfigure.

This isn't magic. It's feedback.

It's the wisdom of crowds - **not the mob**, but the market. Millions of people acting freely, exchanging information through prices, reputation, and results.

It's not designed. It's *discovered.*

And that's what Mises meant when he said:

"The market system is a daily plebiscite. Every cent spent is a vote."

What This Means for the Modern World

Here's the takeaway.

Today's challenges - climate change, education, inequality, healthcare - are real. And the temptation to centralize solutions is stronger than ever.

But we must resist it.

Not because we hate government, but because **we love people.**

Real solutions come from:

- Empowering local experimentation.
- Protecting individual choice.
- Encouraging feedback loops.
- Rewarding excellence through free exchange.

That doesn't mean no government. It means **government as a referee, not a ringleader.**

As Smith put it, the role of the state is to **administer justice, protect property, and provide a few basic public goods.** Beyond that, **let people act. Let value emerge. Let innovation breathe.**

The Danger of Forgetting

When central planning rises again - as it inevitably does in new clothes - it will promise progress, fairness, justice.

But remember: **control costs freedom. And it rarely delivers what it promises.**

Even the smartest algorithm cannot replace the dignity of a person making their own decisions, learning from failure, and choosing a better life.

Mises saw that in 1920.

We must see it now.

Chapter 10: Incentives Are the Language of Reality

How Rewards and Penalties Shape Behavior, Build Systems, and Reveal Truth

Imagine two teachers.

Both are brilliant. One works in a classroom where effort is rewarded, ideas are valued, and students are free to succeed or fail based on their own merit. The other works in a system where everyone gets the same grade, no matter how hard they try.

Over time, which teacher thrives? Which one cares more, pushes harder, improves faster?

And now flip the question.

What happens to the students?

This chapter is about **incentives** - the quiet, constant, inescapable forces that shape behavior, drive outcomes, and expose the *true logic* of any system, no matter how noble its stated goals.

Adam Smith and Ludwig von Mises didn't just understand incentives - they built their entire worldview around them. Because once you grasp that people respond to the structure of rewards and penalties around them, you stop being surprised by *what people do* - and start asking *why they do it*.

This is the turning point in our journey: where morality meets mechanism, where principle meets practice. And where a better world begins - not with sermons, but with systems designed to **reward the good and discourage the bad.**

Incentives: The Unwritten Code Behind Every Choice

At its core, an incentive is just a **reason to act**.

You brush your teeth because you want fresh breath. You save money because you fear a rainy day. You call your friend back because you value the relationship - or want to avoid awkward guilt.

We often think of incentives in economic terms - salaries, taxes, bonuses. But incentives go far deeper. They include:

- **Social incentives:** praise, shame, peer pressure, admiration.
- **Moral incentives:** guilt, pride, conscience.
- **Structural incentives:** rules that make one option easier than another.

Every decision you make - consciously or not - is shaped by some combination of these.

Mises recognized this and built his theory of *praxeology* - the science of human action - around it. Smith, for his part, viewed the moral sentiments as a kind of **internal incentive structure**, where people strive to be seen as "lovely" by others.

Together, they offer a profound truth:

Behavior is rarely random. It's responsive. Change the incentives, and you change the outcome.

The Seen and Unseen Incentive

Let's return to Bastiat's principle from the previous chapter - *the seen and the unseen.*

Every policy creates **visible rewards** and **invisible consequences**. That includes incentives.

Example:

A government subsidizes college tuition.

Seen: More people enroll.

Unseen: Tuition rises (because demand is artificially inflated). Students take on debt for degrees with low market value. Universities expand unnecessary departments. The labor market is flooded with similar skill sets.

Why? Because the **incentive** was to attend school - not necessarily to acquire economically valuable knowledge.

This doesn't mean the policy was evil. But it misunderstood the power of incentives.

The same applies to welfare programs that unintentionally penalize work, tax laws that encourage evasion, and corporate bailouts that reward risk-taking without consequences.

When you subsidize something, you get more of it. When you tax something, you get less. When you ignore incentives, you get chaos.

Incentive Loops in Everyday Life

Let's zoom in.

1. In Business:

If bonuses are based on short-term sales, expect short-term thinking - even if it destroys long-term value. If customer service reps are punished for long calls, expect them to hang up early. If CEOs are paid regardless of company performance, expect mediocrity.

2. In Education:

If schools are rewarded for standardized test scores, expect "teaching to the test." If grades are curved, students will compete instead of collaborate. If effort isn't recognized, apathy grows.

3. In Families:

If children get attention only when they misbehave, guess what behavior increases? If parents always give in to tantrums, tantrums become currency.

People aren't broken. Their **systems** are.

Why Good Intentions Aren't Enough

This is where many well-meaning reforms fail.

They assume that changing outcomes is just about **telling people what to do**. But Mises and Smith would caution:

People don't respond to advice - they respond to incentives.

You can tell someone to save money. But if inflation is higher than the savings rate, they won't.

You can tell companies to lower emissions. But if polluting is cheaper than compliance, they won't.

You can tell politicians to be honest. But if reelection depends on pandering or deception, most won't.

So the real question isn't: "What do we want people to do?"

It's: **"What are we rewarding right now without realizing it?"**

The Dark Side: Perverse Incentives

Some of the worst outcomes in history have come not from malice, but from **incentive structures gone wrong.**

- The 2008 Financial Crisis:

Banks were incentivized to issue risky loans because they could sell them off. Credit rating agencies were paid by the firms they rated. Result? A global meltdown.

- The "War on Drugs":

Police departments received funding based on arrests, not outcomes. Prosecutors were rewarded for convictions, not justice. Result? Mass incarceration and broken communities.

- Disaster Relief:

In some cases, humanitarian aid has created dependence, distorted local markets, or fueled corruption - because the **incentives** rewarded distribution, not long-term resilience.

These are not failures of compassion. They are failures of *design*.

Markets Work Because Incentives Align

Here's the genius of free markets: when structured properly, **they align private gain with public good.**

- A business that makes customers happy gets rewarded with profit.
- An employee who adds value gets promoted.
- An inventor who solves a problem gets funded.

No central authority commands this. It happens because the system **lets people pursue their own goals - but in ways that benefit others.**

This is Smith's "invisible hand" in motion.

Mises took it further: in a well-functioning market, profit and loss act like *moral signals*.

- **Profit** tells you: "You're creating value."
- **Loss** tells you: "You're destroying it."

Remove those signals - through bailouts, monopolies, or command economies - and suddenly, bad ideas get rewarded, and good ones are smothered.

Markets aren't perfect. But they *learn*. And that learning happens through incentives.

What About Morality?

Some say, "But shouldn't people do the right thing without needing rewards?"

Yes. In a perfect world.

But as Smith wrote, people are not angels. And as Mises showed, people act in response to what they feel and believe - *not what they're told.*

This doesn't mean we should abandon ethics.

It means we should **design systems that reward ethical behavior** - so doing the right thing also becomes the *smart* thing.

- Want less pollution? Make it costly to pollute.
- Want more innovation? Let inventors keep more of what they create.
- Want better education? Fund students, not just institutions.

Incentives don't replace morality.

They **channel** it.

The Freedom to Choose - And Be Responsible

Ultimately, incentives only matter if people are **free to respond to them**.

That's why coercive systems collapse. They don't allow true feedback. People do what they're told - or what they can get away with - not what they believe is best.

Free societies, by contrast, are noisy. Messy. Unpredictable.

But they're also **adaptive**.

Because when people can choose, they can learn. They can suffer the costs of bad choices - and reap the rewards of good ones. And in that process, they grow.

Which is why the foundation of all good incentives is this:

Freedom. Followed by accountability. Guided by feedback. And shaped by purpose.

What You Can Do

As a citizen, consumer, parent, employee, or entrepreneur, you have a role to play.

- Support policies that reward productivity, not dependency.
- Choose businesses that align profit with principle.
- Give feedback. Vote with your wallet. Tip well. Encourage excellence.
- And most of all, **look at your own life**: What are you incentivizing in yourself and others?

Because the world doesn't change through lectures.

It changes when good behavior becomes not just admirable - but *irresistible*.

PART III:

THE ETHICS OF EXCHANGE

Chapter 11: The Beauty of Voluntary Trade

Why Free Exchange Is a Moral Act - and the Foundation of Prosperity

There is something almost sacred about a simple handshake between two people agreeing to exchange.

No coercion.
No threat.
No manipulation.

Just: *You have something I want. I have something you want. Let's trade.*

That's it.

And in that moment - mundane though it may seem - we find one of the most morally elegant, socially stabilizing, and economically productive forces in human civilization: **voluntary exchange.**

Adam Smith believed that the act of trading wasn't just about profit - it was about *dignity*. It recognized that others have agency, preferences, and the power to say yes or no.

Ludwig von Mises saw it, too: the market is a mechanism of mutual service. Each trade is a vote. Each transaction is a sentence in the ongoing dialogue of human wants and solutions.

In this chapter, we'll explore how voluntary trade uplifts rather than exploits, how it replaces conflict with cooperation, and how it transforms strangers into allies - not through shared ideology, but through *mutual benefit.*

Because in a world as divided as ours, few truths are more vital than this:

You don't need to agree with someone to trade with them. You only need to respect their freedom to choose.

The Myth of the Zero-Sum Game

One of the most common economic fallacies is the belief that if someone gains in a trade, someone else must be losing.

But this isn't poker. It's not war. It's not tug-of-war with limited rope.

Voluntary trade is **positive-sum.** Both sides walk away better off - **or the trade wouldn't happen.**

Imagine buying a sandwich. The vendor values your $8 more than their sandwich. You value their sandwich more than your $8. Both of you gain.

It's so ordinary that we miss the miracle.

Two people with different desires, resources, and goals - each acting freely - improve their well-being by *cooperating*. And this simple dynamic, repeated billions of times across the planet every day, is what creates **prosperity.**

This, Smith noted, is not driven by benevolence - but by interest aligned through exchange. And it works not because people are saints, but because the incentives reward *solving someone else's problem.*

Trade Is Built on Respect

Every time you make a voluntary trade, you affirm something quietly powerful:

- That **other people's preferences matter**.
- That **they own themselves and their labor**.
- That **they are free to say no**.

You can't force someone to trade and still call it voluntary. The moment one side is coerced - by law, threat, or manipulation - the moral foundation collapses.

This is why markets, unlike politics, tend to de-escalate conflict.

In politics, when I win, you lose. In markets, I don't need to defeat you - I just need to serve you.

This doesn't mean every market is perfect. It means that, at their best, markets are **peaceful arenas of negotiation**. They allow people of different faiths, backgrounds, politics, and languages to *collaborate without conformity*.

As long as coercion is absent, trade is **a moral pact of mutual consent.**

The Decency of Specialization

Voluntary trade would be impossible if everyone had to be self-sufficient. Thankfully, we're not. Human beings are **specialists.**

Smith's famous example comes from a pin factory: when workers specialize in different parts of the process - cutting, shaping, polishing - output skyrockets.

Why? Because specialization increases efficiency, skill, and innovation. But it only works if people can trade what they *specialize in* for what they *lack*.

You may be a brilliant coder but a lousy gardener. I may be a fantastic chef but useless with technology. Neither of us suffers - because we can trade.

This is how civilization scales.

Voluntary exchange enables **comparative advantage** - a concept Mises advanced further by showing that even those with fewer resources can still specialize in what they do *least inefficiently*, and benefit from trade.

This is true not just among individuals - but among *nations*.

Trade Doesn't Care About Borders

Let's explode a myth:

Trade between nations is not between countries. It's between *people*.

When an American buys a phone assembled in South Korea, they're not trading with "South Korea." They're trading with a company, employing people, who are solving a problem.

Protectionists often say, "We need to keep jobs at home." But what they really mean is: *we need to prevent people from buying better, cheaper goods elsewhere.*

They frame trade as betrayal.

Smith and Mises would call it *freedom*.

Trade between people in different countries raises standards of living, fosters peace, and creates global networks of interdependence. It reduces the incentive for war. It creates incentives for cooperation.

It's not about loyalty to soil. It's about loyalty to *voluntary choice*.

Voluntary Doesn't Mean Equal Outcomes

Now, let's address a critique: "But not all trades are fair. Sometimes people trade out of desperation."

This is true - and serious.

A poor person might accept a low wage or a bad deal because they lack options. But the cause of that injustice is not **trade itself** - it's the **lack of alternative opportunities**.

What makes trades unfair is not that they happen - it's that *better trades are artificially blocked*.

- When regulations prevent startups.
- When monopolies are protected by political power.
- When cronyism rigs the playing field.

In those cases, the solution is not to **ban trade**. It's to **open the market** - to more participants, more ideas, more innovation.

Voluntary trade is not the enemy of justice.

It's the *pathway* to it - if we protect the freedom to enter, compete, and improve.

Trade and Trust

Earlier, we explored trust and reputation. Here we see it again: **markets run on trust.**

You can't force someone to shop at your store. You must earn their confidence.

That's why fraud is punished in markets. Why repeat customers are gold. Why reviews, ratings, and recommendations matter.

In every healthy marketplace, character compounds.

The more honest you are, the more valuable your reputation. The better your service, the more people return. Trade becomes not just economic - but *relational*.

Even in anonymous online markets, feedback loops create moral pressure: do right - or be exposed.

This is what Smith meant when he said that people, guided by their own interest, often serve others more effectively than when they try to serve them *directly* through centralized planning.

Because markets don't need saints. They just need **systems that reward virtue and reveal value.**

The Morality of Markets

Let's not shy away from the moral core.

Voluntary trade is a **nonviolent interaction**. It says, "I will offer what I have, and you may accept - or not." It requires no conscription, no propaganda, no force.

It presumes that you are capable of choosing for yourself.

That's not just an economic statement. That's a moral one.

It affirms dignity. It rewards service. It encourages feedback. It humbles the arrogant. It empowers the overlooked.

This is why the greatest market economies are also the greatest engines of social mobility, innovation, and cultural diversity.

They don't demand agreement.

They reward *value*.

The Threats to Voluntary Trade

But voluntary trade is under threat.

From those who:

- Mislabel all profit as exploitation.
- Treat trade as war by other means.
- Push regulation that favors incumbents.
- Demand that only "approved" values be allowed in commerce.

These threats are subtle. They come cloaked in justice, fairness, safety.

But what they often do is **replace choice with coercion.**

They remove your ability to decide who you trade with, how, and for what.

And in doing so, they don't eliminate power - they *centralize it.*

Smith warned us about this in his distrust of "men of system." Mises saw it in the expansion of bureaucratic planning.

If trade is no longer voluntary, society becomes a contest of force - not a collaboration of free agents.

What You Can Do

Support voluntary trade in your own life:

- Choose to buy from people who offer value - not just convenience.
- Respect others' right to trade in ways you might not understand.
- Resist calls to politicize every transaction.
- Recognize that free exchange is not just an economic act - it's a vote for peace.

Because in every honest trade, we rehearse the world we want to live in:

- A world where cooperation beats coercion.
- Where strangers become allies.
- Where dignity is not granted by authority - but earned through service.

Chapter 12: Money, Prices, and the Memory of Effort

What Currency Really Represents - and Why It's More Than Just Paper or Code

You've likely held a dollar bill or seen a number in your bank account and thought of it as "money." But pause for a moment and ask - *what is it, really?*

A piece of cotton-blend paper? A digital signal in a database? An IOU from a central bank?

That's the physical shell. But **money's true power** lies in something less tangible and far more profound:

Money is memory.

It records past effort. It represents value created. It captures cooperation across time and space. It is not wealth in itself - it is a placeholder for all the ways we've helped others and can, in turn, ask others to help us.

In this chapter, we'll explore how money emerged organically, how it coordinates billions of decisions, and why inflation, manipulation, or misunderstanding of money can distort the entire moral and economic fabric of a society.

Smith laid the groundwork. Mises built the structure. And if we listen carefully, we'll see how a proper understanding of money can restore both **prosperity and integrity** to the world around us.

From Barter to Currency: The Birth of Money

Let's start at the beginning.

Before money, people **bartered**. A shoemaker traded shoes for milk. A farmer traded eggs for firewood. It worked - barely.

But barter has limits:

- What if the other person doesn't want what you're offering?
- What if values aren't easily matched?
- What if trade needs to happen later, not now?

Enter **indirect exchange** - the beginning of money.

Over time, people began to accept *intermediate goods* not because they needed them, but because they *knew others would*. Beads, shells, salt, and eventually, **precious metals** emerged as common mediums.

Gold wasn't useful for survival - but it was scarce, divisible, portable, durable, and widely desired.

And from that, **money was born.**

It wasn't invented by governments. It **emerged** - organically, spontaneously - from the needs of free people trying to cooperate.

That's the first great insight from Mises: **money is a market phenomenon, not a political one.**

What Prices Really Are

Money alone isn't enough. We also need a system to *compare* things - so we can decide what's worth what.

That's where **prices** come in.

Prices are not arbitrary numbers set by some distant force. They are **signals** - flashes of information generated by millions of voluntary exchanges.

If avocados are expensive, that's not a judgment or injustice. It means:

- They're in high demand.
- Or in short supply.
- Or both.

If prices drop, it means producers are adjusting, technologies are improving, or consumers are walking away.

Prices tell the truth - if they're allowed to.

When governments interfere with prices (through caps, floors, or manipulation), they **distort the truth**. The signals go haywire. Overproduction or shortages result. People make decisions based on illusions, not reality.

Mises understood this acutely. He wrote that prices are the **foundation of economic calculation** - the only way entrepreneurs, workers, and planners can know what to produce, how much, and for whom.

Without real prices, **an economy is like a pilot flying blind.**

Money as Time and Trust

Here's a powerful shift in thinking:

Money is stored time.

When you work, you exchange your time and skills for money. That money can later be exchanged for *other people's time and skills*. You spend a few dollars on lunch? You're tapping into a massive web of labor: farmers, drivers, cooks, janitors, cashiers.

That's not magic. It's **trust**.

You trust that your money will be accepted. That it will hold value. That others will recognize it as legitimate.

Break that trust - through hyperinflation, counterfeiting, or government overreach - and the whole system cracks.

We've seen it happen:

- **Weimar Germany** in the 1920s: people brought wheelbarrows of currency to buy bread.

- **Zimbabwe** in the 2000s: trillion-dollar bills lost value overnight.

- **Venezuela** in the 2010s: collapse of savings, salaries, and sanity.

These weren't just monetary collapses. They were **moral ones** - because people lost the ability to **translate effort into stable value**.

Inflation: The Silent Thief

Inflation doesn't feel like theft. But it is.

It erodes purchasing power quietly. You still have the same dollars - but they buy less. It's like pouring water into wine: the glass looks full, but the flavor disappears.

Smith warned of inflation as a hidden tax. Mises went further, arguing that **inflation distorts the entire economic structure**:

- It misleads entrepreneurs.
- It discourages savings.
- It punishes long-term planning.
- It widens inequality (those close to the money printers benefit first).

In modern economies, central banks control money supply. Their goal is "price stability" - but too often, they respond to political pressure, speculative bubbles, or short-term fears.

When money becomes a tool of policy rather than a measure of value, **truth is lost**.

And without truth, trust dies.

Cryptocurrency: The New Money Frontier?

In recent years, a rebellion against central banking has emerged - **cryptocurrency**.

Bitcoin, Ethereum, and others promise **decentralized, deflationary, borderless money**. No middlemen. No manipulation. Just code, math, and trustless verification.

Mises didn't live to see this, but his ideas helped inspire it.

He argued that **sound money must emerge from the market,** not be dictated by the state. Crypto advocates see digital currency as a return to that vision: money as *choice*, not coercion.

But crypto also faces challenges:

- Volatility.
- Scalability.
- Regulatory uncertainty.
- Moral ambiguity (used for crime, speculation).

Still, it reflects a crucial truth: **when people lose faith in traditional money, they seek alternatives.**

That search is not dangerous.

It's *inevitable.*

Why Honest Money Matters

We often treat money as neutral. A tool. A background detail.

But money is **moral infrastructure**.

- It enables cooperation among strangers.
- It protects effort from decay.
- It lets value travel through time.

When money is honest - backed by scarcity, trust, and transparency - **it rewards virtue**:

- Save today? Prosper tomorrow.
- Work hard? Build wealth.
- Serve others? Earn freely.

But when money is distorted, it does the opposite:

- Savings are punished.
- Risk is subsidized.
- Debt is cheapened.
- Bubbles grow.

And worst of all, **those closest to the spigot gain unfairly**, while ordinary people lose ground.

Smith warned that inflation favors "projectors" (speculators) over workers. Mises showed how manipulation of money leads to **business cycles** - booms and busts driven not by real growth, but by artificial credit.

Honest money is not a luxury.

It's the **precondition for justice** in a market society.

The Future of Money Is the Future of Freedom

So what should we hope for?

Not a return to barter. Not rigid systems that prevent innovation. But a world where:

- People can **choose their currency**.
- Governments **protect purchasing power**, not dilute it.
- Prices **signal truth**, not ideology.
- Money is **earned, not conjured**.

This future isn't about gold vs. fiat, dollars vs. Bitcoin. It's about a *philosophy*:

That the effort you give today should not vanish tomorrow. That your time has meaning. And that the record of your value should be *trustworthy*.

Money, at its best, is not just currency. It is **a sacred contract** between effort and reward, between today and tomorrow, between self and society.

To treat it lightly is to weaken the bridge between people.

To protect it is to honor the work of everyone who's ever traded something good for something better.

Chapter 13: Profits with Purpose

What Capitalism Gets Right - and Why Value Creation is a Moral Act

"Profit" has become a dirty word in many circles.

It conjures images of greedy CEOs, environmental destruction, layoffs, and lavish bonuses. In media and politics alike, profit is often cast as a synonym for exploitation. A sign that someone, somewhere, must be getting hurt.

But what if we've misunderstood the whole picture?

What if profit - *real profit, earned through voluntary exchange and genuine service* - is not a symptom of corruption, but **a signal of value**?

What if, rather than being the enemy of justice, profit is actually **the fuel of human progress**?

In this chapter, we will strip away the myths, decode the morality of markets, and examine why capitalism - at its best - doesn't reward greed. It rewards **service**.

Mises and Smith both saw this clearly. And if we listen with clear eyes and open minds, we can rediscover a truth that could heal much of the economic confusion plaguing our modern world:

Profit is not the problem. It's the prize for solving problems.

What Profit Really Is

Profit, at its simplest, is **the surplus value you create**.

You take raw materials, effort, and insight - and turn them into something people willingly pay more for.

If you sell handmade candles for $20, and your costs are $10, your profit is $10. That $10 isn't theft. It's a reward for:

- Identifying what people want.
- Taking the risk to provide it.
- Investing time and energy to deliver.

Mises would call this "entrepreneurial action." It is not mere capital ownership - it is **the act of anticipating needs and fulfilling them better than others.**

Smith would add a moral layer: **it is a form of cooperation.** You didn't steal your customer's money. They gave it to you - freely, gratefully - because you made their life better.

In that sense, **profit is a signal from society: "You did something well."**

Profit Is Not Greed

Greed is an attitude - an excess of desire, often at the expense of others.

Profit, by contrast, is a **measurement** - a result of transactions where both sides benefit.

Greed can drive profit, yes. But it can also drive *loss*, *corruption*, or *collapse*. Greed, unchecked, leads to bad business practices that get punished in healthy markets - through boycotts, lawsuits, bad reviews, and competition.

In other words:

Greed is not rewarded in capitalism. *Value creation* **is.**

Where profits come from manipulation, lies, or political favoritism, they should be condemned - not because profit is bad, but because **coercion violates the voluntary nature of trade.**

Mises insisted that capitalism must be free of state favoritism. Crony capitalism, he said, is **not capitalism** - it's **privilege** disguised as productivity.

The Moral Genius of Capitalism

Capitalism, properly understood, is a system that turns **self-interest into service**.

If you want to succeed, you must ask:

- What does someone else want?
- How can I deliver it better, cheaper, faster, or more beautifully?
- How can I earn their trust?

You cannot force them to buy. You must convince them.

That is not exploitation. That is **civilization.**

Smith captured this in his iconic line:

"It is not from the benevolence of the butcher, the brewer, or the baker, that we expect our dinner, but from their regard to their own interest."

In other words, **we benefit when others pursue their own goals in ways that align with ours.**

That's not a loophole. That's the *design.*

Profit as Discovery

Here's a deeper truth: **profit is a signal of discovery.**

When you earn profit, it's because you've figured something out that others missed:

- A new way to cut costs without hurting quality.
- A better product at the same price.
- A service that delights people.

Every successful innovation - from sliced bread to smartphones to electric cars - came from **someone noticing what was missing**, and filling that gap better than anyone else.

Profit is how society says: *Thank you. Do more of that.*

Loss, conversely, says: *This didn't help. Try again.*

That feedback loop is how markets learn. It's how society gets smarter. It's how we go from scarcity to surplus, from survival to thriving.

No central planner could ever replicate that process - because **only individuals on the ground know what's working.**

Risk, Reward, and Responsibility

Many people misunderstand profit as "unearned" or "passive." But real profit involves **risk**.

- You launch a product with no guarantee it will sell.
- You quit a stable job to start something new.
- You invest your savings in a venture that could fail.

When it works, you're rewarded. When it doesn't, you lose.

That's the moral symmetry of markets: **no reward without responsibility.**

This is what separates profit from **plunder.** In socialism or corporatism, people gain power or wealth through favoritism, manipulation, or forced redistribution.

In capitalism, success is earned - by **creating more value than you consume.**

Profit is not a payout. It's a scorecard of contribution.

Profit vs. Exploitation

Here's a common objection: "What about sweatshops? Isn't that profit at the expense of people?"

Let's be clear. **Exploitation exists** - but we must distinguish between:

- Voluntary labor under poor conditions (often better than the alternatives).
- And **coerced labor or fraud**, where consent is not real.

Mises argued that **real capitalism uplifts**, because competition forces employers to offer better wages and conditions over time - or lose workers to rivals.

Where that's not happening, the issue is usually **lack of freedom**, not too much of it.

The answer is *not* to ban trade, punish profit, or shut down factories. The answer is to expand access, remove barriers, and let markets work *for* the people who most need better options.

Smith would ask: *Do these people have the freedom to walk away?* If not, the market isn't working - and the solution is **more openness**, not less.

Profit and Purpose

The best businesses today - large and small - understand that **profit is not the opposite of purpose.**

- Patagonia donates profits to environmental causes.
- TOMS Shoes pioneered "one-for-one" giving.
- Local bakeries sponsor school fundraisers.
- Freelancers build careers around solving problems they care about.

These are not anomalies. They're **proof** that when you earn your money honestly, you can use it *meaningfully*.

Profit, then, is not just permission to live well. It's **fuel for purpose**. It allows you to hire, build, give, grow, invest.

It's the **freedom to scale your values**.

And a society that scorns profit cuts off its own oxygen.

What Happens When Profit Is Demonized

When profit is misunderstood or vilified, two things happen:

1. **Good people exit the marketplace.** They feel ashamed for charging fairly, growing their businesses, or seeking success. They stop innovating.

2. **Bad people fill the void.** Cronyists, rent-seekers, monopolists - those who manipulate the system rather than serve it - step in and claim the profits *without* the risk or value creation.

This is the irony of anti-capitalist rhetoric: **it drives out the moral actors, and strengthens the immoral ones.**

Smith feared the same. He distrusted monopolists and "merchants and manufacturers" who colluded with the state. Mises, too, warned of the dangers when the profit motive is replaced by political privilege.

Profit is like fire: *dangerous when misused, but essential for light and warmth.*

Don't extinguish it. **Channel it.**

Your Role in the Profit Equation

You don't have to be a billionaire or business owner to participate.

- Every time you support a local entrepreneur, you're voting for value creation.

- Every time you offer something excellent in exchange for payment, you're contributing to a system that rewards effort and quality.

- Every time you applaud rather than shame honest success, you're upholding the morality of service.

Because capitalism - real capitalism - isn't about what you take.

It's about **what you trade to earn.**

In Praise of the Profitable

So let us reframe profit once and for all.

- Not as greed, but as **gratitude** from the people you serve.
- Not as exploitation, but as **evidence** that you've helped.
- Not as shameful, but as **sacred** - when earned through free and fair exchange.

Because the moment we teach our children that profit is shameful, we teach them that **success through service is suspect**.

And once that belief takes root, we kill the very engine that lifts people out of poverty, fuels innovation, and funds the causes we love.

Let profit be *what it was always meant to be*:

A receipt for value. A reward for risk. A signal of worth. A tool for purpose.

And most of all - a **moral invitation to do more good, better.**

Chapter 14: When Markets Go Wrong

Externalities, Monopolies, and the Moral Limits of Market Systems

Markets, for all their elegance and moral power, are not utopias.

They can fail.

- Pollution can go unpriced.
- Monopolies can stifle innovation.
- Essential workers can be underpaid.
- Products that harm people - addictive, manipulative, or dishonest - can thrive.

If capitalism is a game, sometimes the scoreboard miscounts. Sometimes the rules get rigged. Sometimes the game itself is tilted against those who never had a real chance to play.

This chapter is not a retreat from the ideas of Smith or Mises - it is their natural extension. Because both thinkers acknowledged that markets operate best within **a moral and institutional framework**.

Smith warned about collusion, corporate power, and the limits of self-regulation. Mises, while more skeptical of state intervention, believed that property rights and voluntary cooperation required a **legal and moral structure** to thrive.

So the question is not "Do markets ever go wrong?"

The question is: **What should we do when they do?**

And just as importantly: **How do we intervene without breaking the very system that makes prosperity possible?**

Market Failure #1: Externalities

An **externality** occurs when a transaction affects people who aren't part of it - and their costs or benefits are **not reflected in the price.**

Classic example: pollution.

A factory sells steel at a competitive price. But it dumps waste into a river. That waste harms fishermen, wildlife, and people downstream.

The buyers and sellers of steel don't bear those costs - **others do**.

This is a failure. Not of capitalism itself, but of **price precision**. The full cost of the transaction is hidden. And because price is how markets communicate, a hidden cost is a **form of deception**.

Smith, though writing before the formal concept of externalities, believed that justice required such effects to be corrected. Mises, too, understood that **the rule of law** had to uphold contracts and **prevent harm to others**.

The solution is *not* to ban the factory or vilify business. It is to **price the externality in.** Pollution taxes, tradable permits, or liability laws can internalize costs, restoring honesty to the price system.

Markets only work when prices tell the truth.

Externalities are lies we must correct.

Market Failure #2: Monopolies and Crony Capitalism

Adam Smith, often caricatured as a cheerleader for big business, **distrusted large firms more than he distrusted government.**

He warned:

"People of the same trade seldom meet together, even for merriment and diversion, but the conversation ends in a conspiracy against the public."

He knew that businesses, left unchecked, would often collude to raise prices, limit competition, and rig markets.

Mises also recognized this - but distinguished between **market-created dominance** (temporary, earned, and unstable) and **government-enforced monopoly**, which is **rigid, unjust, and dangerous**.

Here's the difference:

- If Amazon dominates because it offers better service, that's a reward for value. But if it lobbies for regulations that crush smaller rivals, we've crossed into **crony capitalism.**

- If a local hospital grows by offering great care, good. But if it merges with competitors to **eliminate choice**, that's a **danger.**

The key test is **contestability**: Can new players enter the market? Can customers walk away?

If not, power calcifies. Innovation withers. And freedom shrinks.

Markets are only free when people are **free to compete.**

Market Failure #3: Information Asymmetry and Moral Hazard

Markets assume that people know what they're buying.

But what if they don't?

- You take a loan, but the bank hides the terms.
- You eat food, but the label lies.
- You buy insurance, and then act recklessly because someone else bears the cost.

These are **information failures** - and they distort trust.

Moral hazard occurs when someone takes on risk because they **won't suffer the consequences.**

Think of banks that made reckless bets before the 2008 crash - because they expected a bailout.

This is not capitalism. It's **institutionalized irresponsibility.**

Smith believed in transparency. Mises believed in consequence.

When incentives are divorced from accountability, **markets stop reflecting reality - and start rewarding recklessness.**

Solutions?

- Disclosure laws that inform without overregulating.
- Liability rules that ensure consequences.
- Reputation systems that reward honesty and punish deceit.

Markets are moral machines - but they need *honest inputs*.

Market Failure #4: Commodification of the Inappropriate

Markets are great at allocating resources - but **not all resources should be for sale.**

Consider:

- Should organs be bought and sold?
- Should votes be auctioned off?
- Should children be adopted to the highest bidder?

At some point, **we must draw moral lines.** Smith saw commerce as embedded in culture. Mises believed in the primacy of human action - but both men would balk at the **dehumanization** of certain sacred goods.

Markets need **boundaries**, not because commerce is evil - but because *not everything is a commodity.*

And it takes **culture, not just code**, to know where those lines are.

When Intervention Makes Things Worse

Of course, not every market "failure" calls for government intervention.

Many well-meaning fixes create **worse distortions.**

- Rent control leads to housing shortages.
- Minimum wage hikes can price low-skilled workers out of jobs.
- Subsidies create overproduction and misallocation.
- "Too big to fail" bailouts reward moral hazard.

The cure can be worse than the disease - **especially when the intervention targets symptoms, not causes.**

That's why both Smith and Mises called for **humility** in policy.

Markets are complex. Interventions ripple.

Before fixing, ask:

- What's causing the failure?
- Is it a true failure of voluntary exchange?
- Will this fix create worse incentives?
- Could local, decentralized solutions work better?

Sometimes the answer is *no action.*
Sometimes it's *smarter action.*

But never **blind action.**

The Role of Law and Culture

Markets don't exist in a vacuum.

They need **rules** - to define property, enforce contracts, prevent fraud, and resolve disputes. That's the **legal frame**.

But they also need **moral norms** - to guide behavior where the law can't reach.

- A business might legally fire a loyal worker. But should it?
- A company might profit from addictive designs. But should it?
- An entrepreneur might deceive through clever marketing. But should they?

This is the role of **character**, **culture**, and **conscience**.

Markets show us *what is desired.* But only **virtue** can show us *what is right.*

Don't Burn the House - Fix the Wiring

Critics of capitalism often point to its flaws as proof the system should be torn down.

But that's like discovering your sink is leaking and bulldozing your house.

No system is perfect. But markets - when paired with institutions of trust, culture, and accountability - have lifted more people out of poverty, oppression, and isolation than any system in history.

When markets go wrong, **the solution is not less freedom.**

It's **better structure. Smarter incentives. Clearer consequences. More transparency.**

We don't need to abandon markets.

We need to **discipline them - without destroying them.**

When Markets Fail Us - We Must Not Fail Markets

Let us not confuse abuse with essence.

A corrupt politician doesn't invalidate democracy. A flawed church doesn't disprove faith. And a dishonest trader doesn't damn capitalism.

Markets are reflections of us.

They amplify who we are. So if we want markets to do better, we must **be better** - as consumers, citizens, creators, and neighbors.

- Demand accountability.
- Reward businesses that uplift.
- Support policies that correct distortion, not punish success.

Because when we get markets right, **they get so much right in return**:

- Innovation.
- Opportunity.
- Choice.
- Mobility.
- Dignity.

And most of all - **peaceful cooperation** among free people.

Chapter 15: Inequality vs. Injustice

Drawing the Right Battle Lines Between Difference and Moral Failure

Let me begin with a truth that is both obvious and uncomfortable:

Inequality is natural. Injustice is not.

Those two ideas are often confused - especially in political discourse, where *difference* is framed as *evil*, and any unequal outcome is treated as evidence of a broken system.

But if you pause, reflect, and strip away the rhetoric, you'll find this:

- Inequality of **talent**, **preference**, **risk appetite**, and **timing** is inevitable.

- Inequality that results from **fraud**, **violence**, or **systemic exclusion** is injustice.

They are not the same.

Adam Smith and Ludwig von Mises both recognized this vital distinction. Smith saw that free people, guided by sympathy and market exchange, will naturally produce a wide range of outcomes. Mises saw that when voluntary trade governs the economy, inequality reflects not oppression - but **diverse individual choices**.

So the question is not "How do we make everyone equal?"

The real question is:

"How do we ensure that differences in outcome come from differences in effort, values, and luck - not from differences in access, rigging, or rights?"

Let's draw that line clearly.

The Fact of Human Difference

Start with what we all know, but are often afraid to say out loud:

- People are born with different abilities.
- Some are more disciplined. Some are more impulsive.
- Some have parents who read to them. Some have parents who don't.
- Some take risks. Some crave safety.
- Some live in cities of opportunity. Some are born into dysfunction.

This is the *human condition.*
And when people are free, those differences compound.

One person invests. Another spends. One studies. Another sleeps in. One builds a business. Another chooses a stable job. These aren't moral judgments - they're just **different paths**, yielding different results.

Inequality, in this light, is **what happens when freedom meets reality.**

Smith understood this well. He believed justice wasn't about *outcomes* - it was about *rules*. Give everyone the same shot at the starting line, and let life play out.

But Mises added a sharper insight: **inequality in a market system doesn't mean the rich always win.** In fact, markets constantly **reshuffle the deck**.

Just look at the past 50 years:

- Sears was once unstoppable. Now it's gone.
- Blockbuster dominated. Then Netflix ate its lunch.
- Young tech founders - nobodies yesterday - are billionaires today.

In capitalism, **inequality is dynamic**. In statism, **it calcifies.**

The problem is not *that some people have more*. It's *how* they got it - and whether others can rise, too.

When Inequality Becomes Injustice

Now let's be clear: **some inequality is immoral.**

- When systems prevent people from competing fairly.
- When corruption rewards connections instead of competence.
- When discrimination blocks access to jobs, housing, or education.
- When elites rig tax codes, regulations, or bailouts to preserve their dominance.

That is not capitalism.

That is **injustice disguised as economics.**

And both Smith and Mises condemned it.

Smith worried deeply about cronyism - the collusion between merchants and governments. He warned that regulation often benefits the *already powerful*, by raising barriers for small players.

Mises echoed that sentiment. He argued that **free markets are the *enemy* of entrenched power**, because they constantly test value and reward change.

When justice is absent, inequality is **frozen** - and that's when resentment becomes justified.

Envy vs. Empathy

We must also face a darker force: **envy.**

Not the desire to have more - but the desire to see *others have less.*

Envy doesn't want justice. It wants *leveling.* It doesn't care if someone earned their wealth honestly - it just resents that they have it.

Smith, again, saw this clearly. He wrote of the "corruption of our moral sentiments" - when we admire the rich simply for being rich, or hate them *simply for being rich.*

Moral maturity means we can hold two thoughts at once:

1. **We want everyone to have the chance to thrive.**

2. **We do not hate those who already have.**

The goal is not uniformity. It is **mobility**.

We should care less about the gap between rich and poor, and more about **whether the poor can become rich** - and whether the rich must keep serving others to stay rich.

That's the moral genius of the market: **profit is never guaranteed.** It must be *earned again, every day*.

Relative vs. Absolute Inequality

Here's a critical distinction almost always missed in public debate.

- **Relative inequality** is the difference between people.

- **Absolute inequality** is the quality of life for the worst off.

You could have a society where everyone earns $50,000 a year. Or a society where some earn $50,000, some $500,000, and some $5 million. Which is more equal?

The first, obviously.

But what if, in the second society, **everyone has clean water, smartphones, long lives, and safe homes** - and in the first, people live in stagnation?

That's the tradeoff.

Capitalism creates **absolute improvement** across the board - but with wider gaps. The rich get richer, yes. But so do the poor, the middle, and the forgotten.

Mises put it bluntly: **without the pursuit of profit, there would be less innovation, less productivity, and fewer goods for all.**

Smith would nod and say: "And that innovation doesn't come from nobles. It comes from the tradesmen, the merchants, the makers."

If we chase *equality of income* at the cost of *equality of opportunity*, we lose *both*.

The Danger of Forced Equality

What happens when a society decides that **equality of outcome** is the goal?

History answers clearly:

- In Maoist China, teachers were executed for being "elitist."
- In Stalin's USSR, farmers were killed for owning too much land.
- In modern Venezuela, price controls meant to "equalize access" led to starvation.

Envy in policy form becomes **destruction.**

When governments try to eliminate inequality through force, they **don't raise the bottom.** They **cut down the top.**

- Talent flees.
- Innovation dies.
- Growth stalls.
- Corruption replaces competition.

The dream of equality becomes a nightmare of **sameness, stagnation, and suspicion.**

That's not justice.

That's **tyranny in egalitarian drag.**

Real Solutions for Moral Inequality

This doesn't mean we ignore inequality.

It means we focus on the right **problems**, using the right **tools**.

Want more fairness?

- **Improve education access.**
- **Remove barriers to entry for small businesses.**
- **End crony subsidies and tax loopholes.**
- **Decentralize opportunity.**
- **Let innovation flourish at the margins.**

Want more mobility?

- **Protect property rights.**
- **Keep markets open.**

- **Encourage savings and investment.**
- **Reform systems that trap the poor in dependency.**

These aren't slogans. They're **design principles** for a world where freedom produces difference - but not despair.

What You Can Do

Inequality feels big. Global. Untouchable.

But you can make it human again.

- Hire someone with potential, not just pedigree.
- Tip generously when you can.
- Mentor someone without connections.
- Build a business that lifts others.
- Vote for policies that **expand opportunity, not punish success.**

Because the answer to inequality is not resentment.

It's **reciprocity**.

The answer to injustice is not revenge.

It's **reform**.

And the answer to difference is not fear.

It's **freedom** - paired with dignity, fairness, and a moral commitment to **never leave someone behind without a path to rise.**

PART IV:

THE GOOD SOCIETY AND THE PATH AHEAD

Chapter 16: The Morality of Work

Why Labor Is More Than a Paycheck

We live in a culture that often sees work in two extremes:

- As a **burden**, a necessary evil, something we do until we can escape it.

- Or as an **idol**, where productivity becomes identity, and success replaces meaning.

Neither is quite right.

Work is neither a curse nor a savior.

Done well, it's something far more profound.

Work is **how we serve**, **how we grow**, and **how we earn the trust and cooperation of others**. It is an arena where our talents meet the world's needs. It is not just what we *do* - it's often how we *become*.

Adam Smith and Ludwig von Mises both understood work as a **moral activity**, not just a transactional one. They saw labor as purposeful, identity-forming, and community-building.

This chapter explores how free markets dignify labor, how central planning corrodes it, and how the meaning of work must be defended - not just for wages, but for *human worth*.

Because when we lose the value of work, we don't just harm the economy - we **harm the soul.**

What Is Work, Really?

At its core, work is **the effort to transform something - yourself, your environment, or your situation - into something better.**

- A carpenter turns wood into furniture.
- A teacher turns confusion into confidence.
- A coder turns logic into solutions.
- A janitor turns disorder into peace.

Every act of labor, whether celebrated or unseen, is a statement:

"I am capable. I am needed. I can make a difference."

In markets, this difference is rewarded with payment - **not as charity, but as recognition**. Money in this sense is not just income. It's a token of contribution. A receipt that says: *You did something someone else valued.*

And in that exchange lies **dignity**.

Smith on Specialization and Pride

Adam Smith's most famous economic insight was about **specialization** - how dividing labor into narrow tasks increased productivity.

But he wasn't just describing assembly lines. He was also hinting at something deeper: **a society where each person, by mastering a task, could find pride and purpose.**

In *The Wealth of Nations*, Smith warns that over-specialization without education could make workers "as stupid and ignorant as it is possible for a human creature to become." He knew that *work shapes the mind.*

So the solution wasn't to abandon work - but to **surround it with learning, community, and moral growth.**

Work was not just what you *had to do* - it was *how you participated in civilization.*

Mises on Labor as Action

For Mises, work was a specific form of **purposeful human action**.

It was not just motion. It was **choice**, aimed at removing dissatisfaction - through effort.

He made a crucial distinction: work is not always painful. Sometimes we enjoy it. Sometimes we suffer through it. But in all cases, **we engage with the world to improve our standing within it.**

This view restores agency to workers. It says:

- You are not a cog.
- You are not a victim.
- You are not a pawn.

You are an actor, a chooser, a creator of value.

And when labor is voluntary, market-driven, and morally framed, it becomes **a form of self-expression.**

Work and Self-Respect

The late American sociologist Richard Sennett once said that **"respect depends on being seen as a contributor."**

This is a truth markets have long understood.

You don't need a degree or pedigree to earn a living. You need to offer something others value. In that sense, **work is one of the most democratic institutions on earth.**

- The plumber who fixes your leak earns your respect.
- The waitress who gets your order right earns your tip.
- The coder who builds a great app earns your download.

This is not about social status. It's about **earned regard**.

That regard fosters **self-respect**. And self-respect, once earned, is a defense against despair, apathy, and resentment.

When people work, they don't just get income. They get **evidence** that they matter.

When Work Is Undermined

But not all systems honor this dignity.

In planned economies, work is often **assigned**. You don't choose - you are chosen. You don't offer - you comply. The value of your labor is **dictated**, not discovered.

What happens then?

- People lose motivation.
- Excellence fades.
- Corruption grows.
- Pride disappears.

Without free exchange, work becomes a burden again - a tool of the state, not a bridge between people.

This isn't theory. It happened.

- In Soviet factories, workers were paid by quotas, not value. Waste soared.

- In Maoist farms, grain was measured by state targets. Famine followed.

- In command economies, job security was guaranteed - but so was **stagnation**.

The lesson?

Security without agency is prison.

People need more than jobs. They need **work that matters**, measured by results - not ideology.

The Meaning of "A Good Job"

What makes a job good?

Not just pay. Not just benefits.

A good job gives:

- **Challenge**: The chance to grow.
- **Autonomy**: The freedom to act.
- **Respect**: The recognition of effort.
- **Progress**: The ability to get ahead.

These things are **moral goods**, not just economic metrics.

And the best labor systems create the **conditions** for these goods to emerge. They don't guarantee them - but they allow workers to seek, find, and negotiate them.

This is where markets shine.

Because in a free system:

- Bad bosses are punished by turnover.
- Good workers are rewarded by promotion.
- Innovation is incentivized, not punished.

Work becomes **dialogue**, not dictation.

The Future of Work: Dignity in Transition

Today, we face new challenges:

- AI threatens many traditional jobs.
- Remote work changes relationships.
- Gig work blurs the line between job and contract.
- Young people seek "purpose," not just pay.

How do Smith and Mises help us now?

They remind us that **value creation still matters**. That even if the forms of work change, the moral essence doesn't.

- If you solve problems, people will pay you.
- If you serve others, you will be valued.
- If you innovate, you will earn.

The role of society is not to freeze old jobs in place - but to create **flexible institutions** where new forms of labor can emerge with dignity, fairness, and freedom.

Because the real threat is not robots.

It's **systems that disconnect work from worth.**

Your Work Matters

Let's end where we began.

Work is not just toil. It's not just output. It's not just money.

It is the place where **your action meets the needs of others.**
It is how you shape the world - and how the world shapes you.

Whether you sweep floors or write code, bake bread or lead teams - your labor, done freely and well, is **a form of love.**

- Love for craft.
- Love for service.
- Love for family.
- Love for the future.

And when markets function well - when prices are honest, trade is voluntary, and effort is rewarded - **work becomes not just a necessity, but a noble act.**

Let us protect that.

Because the dignity of labor is the dignity of civilization itself.

Chapter 17: Culture, Consumption, and the Myth of Mindless Materialism

Why Buying Isn't the Problem - and What It Reveals About Us Instead

We've all heard the accusation:

"Capitalism turns people into consumers."

We're told we've traded meaning for marketing, values for vanity, depth for dollars.

That we buy things we don't need, with money we don't have, to impress people we don't like.

There's truth in the warning.
But there's also a dangerous oversimplification.

Because what we consume isn't just "stuff."
It's **expression**, **memory**, **identity**, and often - **joy**.

In this chapter, we'll untangle the difference between **consumerism** and **consumption**, between mindless indulgence and meaningful choice.

We'll see how Adam Smith and Ludwig von Mises never glorified greed - but defended the *freedom to value things differently*.

We'll explore how culture shapes what we want - and how what we want *shapes culture in return*.

And we'll ask the harder question:

Is the problem really that people consume too much?
Or that they consume without asking *why*?

The Beauty - and the Bias - of Choice

Walk into any grocery store and you'll see abundance. Thirty kinds of bread. A wall of cereal. Exotic fruits from across the globe.

To some, this is wasteful excess.
To others, it's **civilization**.

Ludwig von Mises saw it this way:

"The market economy… is a democracy in which every penny gives a right to vote."

Every item on that shelf is there because someone, somewhere, *wants* it. That variety isn't a sign of indulgence - it's a sign that human desires are **diverse, evolving, and freely expressed.**

Adam Smith would agree.

He saw consumption not as a moral failure, but as **a mirror of individual preference**. People trade and produce to satisfy wants - and in doing so, they fuel innovation, creativity, and cooperation.

But that doesn't mean all wants are wise.
Or that more choice always means better living.

It means that **we must take responsibility for what we choose - and what it says about us.**

The Myth of the "Mindless Consumer"

The caricature is common:

- The zombie shopper hypnotized by advertising.
- The teenager obsessed with status sneakers.
- The influencer chasing likes through luxury.

140

But this stereotype misses something important:
People buy things for reasons that are often deeper than they seem.

A $200 pair of sneakers might seem frivolous.
But to the kid wearing them in a tough neighborhood, they're a **shield** - a signal of belonging, self-worth, and dignity.

A daily latte might seem like waste.
But to the exhausted parent or overwhelmed student, it's **a moment of control** - a ritual, a comfort.

A fast fashion haul may look like vanity.
But for someone recovering from trauma or hardship, it might be **self-repair**, a step toward confidence.

Mises understood this implicitly in his theory of **subjective value**.

What matters to you *may not* matter to me.
But that doesn't make your preference irrational - it makes it **yours**.

Markets don't judge taste. They reflect it.
And the moral weight lies not in the reflection - but in what we *choose* to see there.

When Consumption Becomes a Crutch

Of course, there is such a thing as **empty consumption** - when buying becomes a substitute for meaning, connection, or identity.

This is the world of:

- Compulsive spending.
- Dopamine-driven retail therapy.
- Social comparison fed by advertising.

And yes - markets can feed this. Algorithms and ad campaigns are now *psychologically weaponized* to keep us scrolling, buying, clicking. And when people feel spiritually hollow or socially isolated, consumption can become **a form of anesthesia**.

But let's be clear: this is not the fault of markets alone.

It's the result of a **cultural vacuum**.

When people lack connection, purpose, or community, they will reach for substitutes.

The solution isn't to restrict choice or shame wealth.

It's to **build better foundations** for meaning - so people don't have to look for it at the mall.

The Role of Culture in What We Want

Markets don't exist in isolation. They're shaped by culture - and they shape culture in return.

- When culture celebrates wisdom, markets produce books, lectures, and podcasts.

- When culture obsesses over youth, markets churn out anti-aging creams and Instagram filters.

- When culture honors sustainability, markets innovate in electric cars and eco-design.

This is key: **Markets don't invent desires - they amplify them.**

Which means that if we don't like what we see in the marketplace, the question is not *"Why is capitalism doing this?"*

It's:

"What are we celebrating? What are we rewarding? What do we admire?"

Smith understood that the moral tone of society is shaped by what we aspire to.

- If we honor virtue, commerce will find ways to serve it.
- If we honor vanity, commerce will deliver that, too.

Markets are not just economic engines. They're **cultural microphones**.

Can Buying Be Beautiful?

Yes.

- A handcrafted chair can honor centuries of craftsmanship.
- A home-cooked meal can celebrate culture and memory.
- A well-made suit can reflect dignity and self-respect.
- A family vacation can create lifelong bonds.

Consumption, when thoughtful, is **a form of stewardship** - of beauty, quality, and human connection.

Smith himself loved fine things. Mises appreciated quality and craftsmanship. Neither man believed that markets should turn people into monks.

They believed, instead, that markets allow **the elevation of taste through experience**. And that over time, people become more discerning - not less.

The more freedom we have, the more **responsibility we bear** to direct our preferences upward.

That is not a market task.

That is a **moral** one.

What About Luxury?

Luxury is often the scapegoat in discussions of inequality. "How can one person buy a yacht when others starve?"

A fair question. But consider this:

- Who builds the yacht?
- Who sells the materials?
- Who maintains it, staffs it, upgrades it?

Luxury, in a free market, is not a withdrawal from the common good - it is a **distribution chain**, fueled by voluntary trade.

When wealth is earned through value creation, **even indulgence can become employment, innovation, and investment.**

And when it's not?
When luxury becomes decadence unmoored from service?

That's a *cultural failure*, not a capitalist one.

A Better Kind of Consumption

So how do we consume without being consumed?

Here's what I believe:

1. **Consume consciously.** Ask: "Does this improve my life - or distract from it?"

2. **Honor quality.** Support goods made with care, not just convenience.

3. **Think downstream.** Who made this? Under what conditions?

4. **Connect spending to values.** What kind of world does this purchase reinforce?

5. **Use markets to tell better stories.** Choose companies, brands, and creators who build up, not tear down.

Because capitalism, when shaped by culture, can do more than sell.

It can **elevate. Inspire. Heal.**

The Marketplace Is a Mirror

The market reflects us.

- Our fears and hopes.
- Our vanities and virtues.
- Our generosity and our insecurities.

To blame markets for what we buy is like blaming a mirror for our expression.

The real question is: **What are we becoming - and are we proud of it?**

Smith and Mises would both agree: **a society that values virtue will create virtuous commerce.** Not by mandate, but by *demand*.

If we want a better market, we must first become **better choosers.**

Chapter 18: The Power of Local

Community, Place, and Decentralized Belonging

Imagine this:

You walk into your neighborhood coffee shop.
The barista knows your name.
The regulars smile in recognition.
The walls hold community art.
The tip jar funds a local charity.
The café owner lives five blocks away.

This isn't just a business.

It's a **node of belonging**.

We've spent much of this book exploring freedom, trade, and morality in broad strokes - global commerce, human action, national policy. But the real test of these ideas is often **hyperlocal**: how they show up in your town, your family, your school board, your corner store.

Smith and Mises didn't use the language of "community" the way we do today. But they deeply understood the power of **decentralization** - that human flourishing happens not through distant authorities, but through **voluntary networks** of trust, accountability, and shared life.

This chapter explores why local matters - why scale is not neutral, why bureaucracy is not benign, and why **freedom without connection can become loneliness**.

Because liberty means little if it doesn't have a **home**.

The Economics of Neighborhood

Let's start with something obvious that we rarely say aloud:

Most of life happens locally.

You don't call Washington when your streetlight goes out.
You don't wait for Brussels to fix your school's roof.
You don't email a senator to resolve a noise complaint.

You turn to people you know.
To institutions you can walk to.
To networks that you can speak into.

Local economies - farmers' markets, barbershops, libraries, restaurants, small businesses - are not just points on a supply chain. They are **living ecosystems of culture, cooperation, and care.**

They matter not because they're small, but because they're **personal.**

Mises believed all action is local in origin - even when the effects ripple globally. Smith understood that trust and sympathy are strongest among those we *see.*

So when policy or commerce forgets the neighborhood, **something human is lost**.

Why Scale Changes Everything

Scale is seductive.

Big companies offer convenience.
Big government offers efficiency.
Big systems offer control.

But every time we scale, we **lose something**:

- **Responsiveness.** Try calling customer service at a telecom giant.
- **Transparency.** Try reading the fine print on a national education bill.
- **Accountability.** Try holding a multinational accountable for pollution in your town.

This is not an anti-big argument. Some things must scale.
But it is a **pro-local** argument.

Because when decisions are made **closer to the people they affect**, they're more likely to reflect real needs, shared values, and honest feedback.

This is what Mises meant when he championed **subsidiarity**:
That no higher authority should do what a lower one can do better.

Freedom isn't just the absence of tyranny. It's the **presence of proximity.**

Community: The Soft Infrastructure of Markets

Markets require more than prices and goods.

They require **relationships**.

Trust, reputation, reciprocity - all the invisible social threads that make trade possible - are **grown in community**.

Think of a small town:

- You can't scam customers. Word gets out.
- You can't ghost your landlord. They see you at church.
- You can't treat workers poorly. Everyone knows someone.

Localism creates a **natural feedback loop**. Not perfect. But faster. More human.

It rewards **character**, not just compliance.

Smith would have called this the "moral sentiments" in action.
Mises would say it's spontaneous order at the community level.

And we know this intuitively:

We behave better when people know our name.

The Fragility of Rootlessness

Modern life is increasingly **placeless**.

We work remotely.
We shop globally.
We socialize digitally.
We vote nationally.

And in that disconnection, many feel unmoored.

- Loneliness rises.
- Mental health erodes.
- Trust in institutions collapses.

The irony? We are more connected than ever, yet less **embedded**.
More efficient than ever, yet less **seen**.

Mises believed in individualism. But not isolation.
Smith celebrated commerce - but also warned that virtue must be
cultivated, not assumed.

And virtue grows in places where people **share life**, not just opinions.

When we lose place, we lose *accountability, empathy,* and *durable belonging.*

Local Isn't Perfect - But It's Personal

Some critics romanticize the local.

- They ignore local corruption.
- They downplay parochialism.
- They forget exclusion.

That's fair.

But the answer to bad localism isn't **centralization**. It's **better localism**.

- Stronger civic norms.
- More open institutions.
- Transparent leadership.
- Economic literacy at the community level.

Because when problems are local, **solutions can be, too**.

And when people have a say where they live, they are more likely to:

- Care.
- Participate.
- Build.

The front porch is a better forum than the federal register.

Decentralized Economics and Distributed Dignity

Mises believed in **entrepreneurial dynamism** - not just from billionaires, but from *anyone* who sees a need and acts.

That spirit lives in:

- Local bakeries experimenting with recipes.
- Mechanics sponsoring high school sports.
- Farmers trying new soil techniques.
- Teachers creating micro-schools.

These aren't just economic acts.
They are **acts of citizenship**.

And they require **room to breathe** - freedom from red tape, from arbitrary mandates, from distant planners who don't know the ground they regulate.

Decentralization isn't just efficient.
It's **ethical**. It restores **the right to solve problems close to home**.

Global Markets, Local Roots

Here's the paradox:

Markets work best when they are **global in opportunity but local in grounding.**

You should be able to:

- Sell worldwide.
- Ship across oceans.
- Collaborate across time zones.

But you should also be able to:

- Know your grocer.
- Trust your plumber.
- Shape your town.

Global capitalism must be balanced by **local connection**.

Smith and Mises wouldn't have opposed the global - they would have insisted that **it must not trample the personal**.

Scale must serve place - not replace it.

What You Can Do

To restore the moral foundation of community, you don't need a policy. You need *presence.*

- Shop local, not just for ethics - but for **relationships**.
- Attend town meetings, even if you're not political.
- Start a local business or support someone who has.
- Mentor someone nearby.
- Share resources in your neighborhood.

Most of all, **root yourself**.

Because freedom isn't floating.

It needs sidewalks. It needs shared rituals. It needs *a place to stand.*

The Market Needs a Neighborhood

In the end, markets are not just systems.

They are **stories** we tell with one another - through trade, trust, and shared life.

And those stories are most alive when we live *among the people we serve.*

Let us honor the local - not with nostalgia, but with **renewed commitment**.

Because freedom without community becomes loneliness. And community without freedom becomes control.

But together?

They become **belonging.**

Chapter 19: The Role of Education

Teaching Choice, Trade, and Character in a Free Society

A free society isn't automatic.

It must be **taught**.

Not through dogma. Not through rote memorization. But through **education that respects agency, encourages discernment, and instills character**.

Because what good is a system built on voluntary action if no one knows how to **choose well**?

Adam Smith and Ludwig von Mises both knew that economic freedom without moral literacy is unstable. That people must learn **not just what is possible - but what is right**.

This chapter is not a policy proposal. It is a **reframing** of what education is for.

Not to mold compliant workers.
Not to manufacture test scores.
But to raise human beings capable of **seeing clearly, deciding wisely, and living freely**.

Education as Formation, Not Just Information

We often reduce education to job prep:

- "Will this help me get a good salary?"
- "Will this look good on a résumé?"
- "Will this get me into the right college?"

But education, in its richest sense, is not just about **data transfer**. It's about **formation**:

- Of habits.
- Of intellect.
- Of taste.
- Of judgment.
- Of *character*.

Adam Smith began his career not as an economist, but as a **moral philosopher**. He believed that sympathy, imagination, and personal reflection were essential ingredients of a good life. And he believed education must foster them.

Mises agreed: a free society depends on people who can understand complexity, weigh tradeoffs, and think for themselves.

Because without that, liberty turns into noise.
Or worse - into license without responsibility.

What Should We Be Teaching?

Here's a question most school systems never seriously ask:

What do people need to know to live well in a free society?

Let's answer it.

1. How to Make Choices

Freedom means nothing if people fear decision-making.

- Teach **opportunity cost** early. Show that every choice has a tradeoff.
- Teach **marginal thinking** - how each additional action brings more or less benefit.

- Teach **long-term thinking** - how actions compound over time.

Smith called this developing "prudence." Mises saw it as foundational to rational action.

Choice is not chaos.
It is character under pressure.

---

2. How to Respect Others' Choices

This is central.

Freedom means your neighbor will sometimes choose things you wouldn't. Different lifestyles. Different values. Different paths.

Education must instill the ability to:

- **Disagree without dehumanizing.**
- **See from others' perspectives.**
- **Coexist without control.**

This is the moral root of voluntary trade.

Smith's "impartial spectator" is born in classrooms where **difference is not feared, but explored.**

---

3. How Trade Works - and Why It Matters

Everyone participates in the economy, but almost no one is taught **how it actually functions**.

- How markets coordinate knowledge.
- How prices emerge from voluntary exchange.
- How profit signals value.

- How incentives shape outcomes.

These aren't just economic ideas.
They are tools for **reading the world.**

Imagine a generation of students who can look at a price, a product, or a protest and ask:

- "What are the incentives here?"
- "Who's choosing what?"
- "Where is value being created - or destroyed?"

That's not just financial literacy.
It's **civic literacy**.

---

4. How to Fail, Reflect, and Try Again

Free societies don't guarantee success.

They guarantee **the right to try** - and the chance to **learn from failure**.

But schools often penalize mistakes so harshly that they become traumatic.

Mises would object. So would Smith.

Because markets *depend* on trial and error.

Growth *requires* feedback.

Education must normalize:

- Failure as feedback.
- Resilience as a skill.
- Adaptation as virtue.

Every entrepreneur fails.
Every moral life includes regret and recovery.

If schools don't teach that, they teach **fear** instead of **freedom**.

---

5. How to Weigh Tradeoffs - Not Chase Perfection

Markets work not because they offer perfect solutions, but because they offer **better ones** - incrementally, adaptively, iteratively.

Education should do the same.

- Don't teach "right answers" - teach **better answers, given your goals and constraints**.

- Don't punish ambiguity - **train discernment.**

Students must learn how to live in a world where:

- Every policy has a cost.
- Every decision has an upside and a downside.
- Every system includes imperfection.

That's not pessimism.

That's **realism with moral clarity.**

Who Should Do the Teaching?

One of the great tragedies of modern schooling is how centralized it has become.

Mises would have recoiled at federal control of education. Smith would have worried about **uniform curricula imposed from above**.

Why?

Because one-size-fits-all education **kills innovation, suppresses local values, and disrespects families.**

Instead, both would argue for **pluralism**:

- Let parents choose schools that match their values.
- Let educators experiment with models.
- Let communities build systems that reflect their needs.

This isn't chaos. It's **entrepreneurial education.**
It's how we discover what works - without sacrificing what matters.

Education and Social Mobility

Let's now talk justice.

Education is often framed as the great equalizer. But that promise is hollow if:

- Systems trap poor kids in failing schools.
- Bureaucracy punishes innovation.
- Credentials matter more than competence.

In a free society, **talent must rise.**
And for that to happen, education must:

- Be accessible.
- Be rigorous.
- Be **open to alternatives.**

Smith and Mises would both say: the best system is one where **value is rewarded - not pedigree.**

That means apprenticeships. Skill-based hiring. Entrepreneurial paths. Charter schools. Online courses. Self-taught expertise.

A diploma should **not** be a gatekeeper to dignity.

Teaching Character in a Secular World

You've asked that this book remain secular.
Rightly so.

But character is not inherently religious.

It is **moral orientation toward the good** - through honesty, discipline, courage, humility, and justice.

Smith believed character emerged through habits, feedback, and social mirroring. Mises believed in the ethical obligations of free individuals to act purposefully and responsibly.

Education must reclaim this:

- Not through moralizing.
- Not through politicized virtue signals.

But through **example, reflection, and real consequence.**

Let students see that their choices affect others.
Let them practice judgment.
Let them learn from mentors who model integrity.

That is not indoctrination.
It is **preparation for freedom.**

What You Can Do

Education doesn't only happen in classrooms.
It happens in homes, offices, churches, streets, screens, and stores.

You can:

- Teach economic literacy to your kids.
- Model ethical entrepreneurship.
- Mentor someone in your trade.
- Volunteer at schools that foster innovation.
- Vote for policies that support parental choice and pluralism in learning.

But above all - **keep learning yourself.**
Because in a free society, the learner is never finished.

The Point of Teaching

Smith believed in sympathy. Mises believed in self-direction. Both believed that **a good society requires good people - formed through practice, not just principle.**

The purpose of education is not to fill heads.

It's to **shape hearts and sharpen minds** - so people can act wisely, serve freely, and participate meaningfully in the beautiful, messy thing we call freedom.

Let us not forget:

The future is not written by institutions. It is written by people who've been taught how to choose well.

Chapter 20: Rights, Responsibilities, and the Ethics of Liberty

Why Freedom Only Works When Paired with Moral Restraint

In the modern world, the word **"rights"** is everywhere.

We demand them.
We legislate them.
We march for them.
We sue over them.

But rarely do we ask the deeper question:

What are rights for - and what must they be *paired with* to mean anything at all?

Because rights, on their own, are incomplete.
In fact, **a society obsessed with rights but ignorant of responsibilities is doomed to crumble under the weight of its own contradictions.**

This was something Adam Smith understood as a moralist.
And something Ludwig von Mises championed as an economist and philosopher of liberty.

Rights are not licenses to do whatever we want.

They are **invitations to act well under freedom**.
And they only work when we're prepared to carry the **burden of liberty** - with restraint, accountability, and purpose.

This chapter explores what that means.

Rights: Shields Against Coercion

Let's begin with what rights *are not*.

Rights are not:

- Promises of outcomes.
- Guarantees of success.
- Claims to other people's labor.

They are **protections** - shields against **interference** from others, especially from the state.

- Your right to speak means no one can punish you for your opinions.
- Your right to property means no one can take what's yours without consent.
- Your right to associate means you can gather with whom you choose.

Mises called these the **preconditions of a liberal society** - not in the partisan sense, but in the classical, liberty-based sense.

Smith agreed: a just society must **protect the negative rights** of individuals - the right *not* to be harmed, *not* to be coerced, *not* to be stolen from.

These rights allow the market, community, and conscience to function without force.

But without *responsibility*, even these become dangerous.

Responsibilities: The Moral Counterbalance

Every right creates a **moral obligation** in someone else.

If I have the right to free speech, you have the responsibility not to silence me.

If I have the right to property, you must not steal or destroy it.

But the deeper responsibilities are **internal**:

- To use our freedom **ethically**.
- To speak **truthfully**, not destructively.
- To consume **wisely**, not wastefully.
- To work **honestly**, not opportunistically.
- To vote **thoughtfully**, not tribally.

This is where liberty matures.

It stops being about **permission** and starts being about **purpose.**

Why Liberty Requires Restraint

Mises warned of this repeatedly:
A free society cannot survive unless its citizens **internalize limits**.

"Freedom means responsibility. That is why most men dread it." - George Bernard Shaw (a quote Mises often referenced)

This is the paradox:

- Freedom **from** coercion requires freedom **within** ourselves.
- Laws cannot cover every case. Markets cannot fix every failure.
- Only **conscience** - the self-governing moral compass - can keep liberty from unraveling into chaos.

Smith believed this conscience was trained through habits, social feedback, and the "impartial spectator" within us.

Mises believed people, if truly rational, would learn that **self-restraint is in their own best interest.**

And both men knew:

Liberty is not sustainable if the free don't act like adults.

Freedom Misused

Let's not pretend liberty always leads to virtue.
It doesn't.

People use freedom to:

- Exploit loopholes.
- Manipulate systems.
- Harass, degrade, deceive, and divide.
- Feed addictions.
- Evade duty.

This is where critics of freedom gain ground.
They say, "See? People can't be trusted. Let's take away their freedom for their own good."

But Mises would answer:

"No. Restrain the abuser, not the principle."

Just as we don't ban cars because some people drive drunk, we shouldn't ban choice because some people choose poorly.

Instead, we build:

- **Consequences** for misconduct.
- **Education** for wise decision-making.
- **Culture** that celebrates virtue over vice.

Liberty as a Moral Discipline

To live freely is to accept that **no one is coming to save you.**
You must:

- Manage your time.
- Shape your habits.
- Navigate tradeoffs.
- Apologize when wrong.
- Forgive others when wronged.
- Cooperate without coercion.

This is **exhausting** sometimes.

But it is also the only known path to **dignity without domination**.

Smith and Mises both saw that **self-direction is the essence of humanity**.

To be fully human is to act - not under command, but under **conscience**.

Rights Without Responsibility Lead to Tyranny

Now here's the danger.

When people assert rights **without** accepting responsibilities, society eventually compensates by installing **external control**.

- If property isn't respected, we get surveillance and confiscation.
- If speech is weaponized, we get censorship.
- If businesses exploit, we get crushing regulation.

People demand safety from the consequences of others' irresponsibility - and so **liberty erodes**, bit by bit.

It's not a conspiracy.

It's a **reaction to freedom misused**.

And so the very people shouting "my rights!" sometimes usher in the regimes that will **take those rights away** - for everyone.

Where Law Ends and Morality Begins

Here's the honest truth:

You can't legislate character.

No law can make someone kind, honest, humble, generous, or patient.

Markets can reward virtue in some cases.
Communities can encourage it.
Laws can deter abuse.

But **only you** can choose to act well when you could get away with something less.

Mises called this the **moral foundation of liberal society**:

That the individual is not just legally free, but **morally capable.**

Smith called it the cultivation of virtue in everyday life.

And together, they challenge us:

If you want to keep your rights, act in a way that earns them.

How to Live Liberty

So what does this look like?

1. **Defend the rights of others - even when you disagree with them.**
   If your neighbor can be silenced, so can you.

2. **Vote as if your grandchildren will live with the outcome.**
   Because they will.

3. **Speak freely - but with discipline and dignity.**
   Because the goal is not just freedom of speech, but freedom *through* speech.

4. **Work with excellence - even when no one is watching.**
   Because work is self-respect in motion.

5. **Give, build, serve - without waiting for permission.**
   Because the world changes by those who take initiative.

Freedom is not **just your right to act**.
It's your **obligation to act rightly.**

Liberty as a Legacy

We often think of liberty as something we **inherit**.

But it's something we must **re-earn** - in every generation.

It requires:

- Teaching our children the value of choice and the burden of consequence.
- Building institutions that trust people - but also hold them accountable.
- Resisting the temptation to outsource our judgment to "experts," "systems," or "saviors."

Because no constitution, no platform, no algorithm can preserve liberty on its own.

Only **character can**.

And that character must be **chosen. Taught. Modeled. Defended.**

Every day.

Freedom's Final Test

The ultimate test of liberty isn't what it gives you.

It's **what it asks of you.**

- Will you use your voice to divide - or to elevate?
- Will you use your wealth to flaunt - or to build?
- Will you use your rights to demand - or to serve?

Smith and Mises knew that a free society depends on free people who act like **stewards**, not just claimants.

Let us meet that test.

With courage.
With clarity.
And with commitment to a world where freedom is not a loophole - but a **light**.

PART V:

MAKING MODERN LIFE MEANINGFUL AGAIN

Chapter 21: The Case for Voluntary Cooperation Over Forced Unity

Why Real Community Emerges From Freedom - Not Force

In an age where unity is often demanded, legislated, or enforced, we rarely ask a deeper question:

Can people truly be united if they are not free to disagree, depart, or dissent?

There is a growing temptation - on both the political left and right - to believe that **harmony must be imposed**. That consensus is too important to be left voluntary. That the risk of division justifies coercion.

But Adam Smith and Ludwig von Mises would have disagreed completely.

They saw that **the most enduring cooperation is voluntary** - rooted in shared interest, mutual respect, and peaceful exchange. Not enforced sameness.

This chapter explores the difference between **consensus and conformity**, between **collective strength and centralized control**.

Because what binds a free society together is not that everyone agrees - It's that everyone agrees **not to force each other to agree.**

The Myth of Unity Through Power

Many political movements claim:
"If we just had the right leader, the right plan, the right rules - then we'd finally be united."

But history tells a darker story.

- In Soviet Russia, unity meant silence under surveillance.
- In Maoist China, unity meant slogans, loyalty checks, and persecution.
- In fascist regimes, unity meant obedience, nationalism, and fear.

This is not **cooperation**.
It is **compliance** under pressure.

It may create temporary order.
But it cannot create **trust**, **joy**, or **creativity**.

Mises saw this clearly: coercion suppresses dissent - but also **discovery**. It punishes the minority that might have the idea that changes everything.

Smith would add: a society that seeks peace by silencing difference loses the **moral empathy** that gives its freedom meaning.

Real unity is not **forced sameness.**

It is **diverse people choosing to live and work together anyway.**

Voluntary Cooperation: How Markets Model It

The market economy is not just an economic tool.
It is a daily rehearsal of **voluntary cooperation**.

- The grocer doesn't know your politics - but they'll still sell you apples.
- The engineer may not pray like you - but she'll still build the bridge.
- The restaurant owner may vote differently - but he'll still make your lunch.

You don't need to *agree* to cooperate.
You just need to *respect each other's right to choose.*

Mises believed this was the great moral genius of capitalism:

It aligns self-interest with service - and turns difference into value.

In a market, people coordinate their plans **not by force, but through signals, negotiation, and feedback.** The price system is a way to **reconcile needs without conflict**.

And it works precisely because it doesn't require **shared beliefs** - only **shared rules**.

The Difference Between Community and Collectivism

People long for connection. That's good.
But there's a critical difference:

- **Community** is chosen.
- **Collectivism** is imposed.

In a community, you can:

- Exit.
- Disagree.
- Negotiate.
- Contribute voluntarily.

In collectivism, you **must comply** - even when your conscience protests.

Smith saw real community as **moral space**, not political space. Mises warned that collectivism always ends up suppressing the individual - because it cannot tolerate deviation.

The true test is this:

Can I say no - and still be safe? Still be heard? Still be welcome?

If not, it's not community. It's a **machine**, and you are just a gear.

Diversity Without Division

Freedom doesn't mean chaos.

It means that **diversity of thought, background, and preference** can exist **without violence, coercion, or fragmentation.**

That's not automatic.
It requires:

- Institutions that resolve conflict peacefully.
- Cultural norms that reward civility.
- Economic systems that turn difference into specialization, not resentment.
- Education that teaches empathy and negotiation, not ideological warfare.

Smith believed humans are social creatures - driven by the desire to be "lovely" to others.
Mises saw that social cooperation under markets expands tolerance by turning **other people's success into your own opportunity.**

In other words:

The freer the society, the less we have to agree - because we don't have to control each other.

When Cooperation Becomes Coercion

Sometimes, "cooperation" becomes a code word for:

- "Fall in line."
- "Support the cause."
- "Agree - or be labeled dangerous."

We see this today:

- Cancel culture weaponizes consensus.
- Corporate activism demands alignment.
- Legislation encodes specific worldviews into law.

These may emerge from good intentions. But they **erode the very trust they claim to protect.**

Because cooperation built on coercion always backfires:

- People hide their real views.
- Creativity dies.
- Resentment festers.
- Eventually, backlash erupts.

Mises warned that the urge to centralize - to control difference - would destroy the ability to **solve problems locally, creatively, and peacefully.**

Smith would call it a **moral failure of imagination**.

How Voluntary Cooperation Builds Stronger Societies

Let's be clear: freedom doesn't eliminate conflict.
It teaches us **how to live with it** - and grow through it.

Voluntary cooperation fosters:

1. **Resilience**

   People can adapt without waiting for permission. Bottom-up solutions flourish.

2. **Innovation**

   Diverse minds solve problems differently. Trade lets them collaborate.

3. **Peace**

   No need to conquer others to win. Just offer a better deal.

4. **Moral Agency**

   Helping others becomes real when it's not mandatory. Giving is a choice, not a tax.

5. **Trust**

   When people act freely and predictably, **social capital increases**.

This is not utopia.

It's simply what happens **when force is restrained and freedom is respected**.

Can Unity Be a Byproduct, Not a Goal?

Here's the twist:

Unity is strongest when it's not the goal - but the byproduct of shared endeavor.

You don't force a team to bond.
You give them a challenge - and they bond **through** it.

You don't legislate friendship.
You work together. Build together. Disagree - and still show up.

That's what markets teach us every day.

And that's why Smith and Mises both saw **commerce as a peace process**.

Because it allows:

- Muslims to trade with Christians.
- Liberals to hire conservatives.
- Young to serve old.
- Foreigners to partner with locals.

Not because they share everything.

But because they **share enough** to make something better - *together*.

What You Can Do

In your life, you can:

- **Invite difference.** Work with people you disagree with. Learn from them.

- **Refuse coercion.** Speak out when unity is demanded at the expense of freedom.

- **Build bottom-up.** Start things - clubs, companies, projects - that rely on voluntary buy-in.

- **Celebrate pluralism.** Don't just tolerate difference. See it as **a feature, not a flaw**.

- **Show up for people, not ideologies.** Because people are where community begins.

Let others chase unity through power.

We'll build it through *freedom, trust,* and *shared humanity.*

Freedom Is the Highest Form of Fellowship

Let me leave you with this:

Unity imposed is fragile.
But cooperation chosen is **resilient.**

It is not loud.
Not sweeping.
Not coercive.

It is quiet, local, human. And it is the *only* kind that endures.

Chapter 22: The Temptation of Utopia - and the Wisdom of Limits

Why Chasing Perfection Can Destroy What Actually Works

At some point, most of us have dreamed of a perfect world.

- No poverty.
- No crime.
- No inequality.
- No pollution.
- No conflict.

A world without scarcity. Without suffering. Without tradeoffs.

It's a beautiful dream.

And a dangerous one.

Because history has shown - repeatedly - that the pursuit of **utopia by force** often leads not to peace, but to **ruin**.

This chapter explores why Mises and Smith both rejected utopian schemes - not out of cynicism, but out of **deep respect for reality, human dignity, and moral humility.**

We'll examine why imperfection is not a failure to fix, but a **fact to live wisely within**. And why limits - far from being oppressive - can be the very things that **protect freedom, foster innovation, and preserve peace.**

What Is Utopian Thinking?

Utopianism isn't just optimism. It's something more rigid:

It's the belief that with the right system, leader, or ideology, we can eliminate all conflict, inequality, suffering, or error.

It says:

- "Once we educate everyone, crime will vanish."
- "Once we equalize outcomes, envy will disappear."
- "Once we automate work, people will flourish."
- "Once we abolish markets, there will be no greed."

It is the assumption that all human flaws are **design flaws** - and can be engineered away.

It is the refusal to accept **tradeoffs**, and the rage at reality when they persist.

Utopianism turns real people into clay - and society into a laboratory.

Mises warned: "The planner sees himself as a god."
Smith would add: "And forgets the people he plans for are not machines."

The Utopian Track Record: Tragedy in Motion

The 20th century was littered with utopian experiments.

- **Communist Russia** promised a worker's paradise. It delivered gulags and famine.

- **Maoist China** declared an end to class and poverty. It delivered mass starvation and terror.

- **Cambodia under the Khmer Rouge** tried to erase all inequality. It erased a quarter of the population.

These were not just policy errors.

They were **moral catastrophes** - driven by the belief that humans could be reshaped like steel if the ideology was pure enough.

Mises predicted this. He warned that **central planning without prices** would lead to **chaos**, because it destroyed the informational fabric of society.

Smith predicted it morally. He said no one can - or should - try to **reshape human nature** through force.

The tragedy of utopia isn't that it fails to deliver perfection.
It's that it destroys *what already works* in the name of something that never will.

Utopianism in Disguise: When Idealism Becomes Control

Modern utopianism often wears new clothes:

- "Universal Basic Income will solve all social issues."
- "Green energy transition must happen by force, regardless of cost."
- "Tech platforms can eliminate misinformation - just trust the algorithm."
- "Equality of identity is more important than equality before the law."

None of these ideas are evil in themselves.

But when they become **non-negotiable**, **impervious to feedback**, or **disconnected from real tradeoffs**, they **drift into utopian territory**.

You'll know it's happening when:

- Questions are treated as threats.
- Dissenters are silenced.
- Tradeoffs are denied.
- Human complexity is ignored.

Mises called this **the fatal conceit**: that a planner knows better than millions of people acting freely.

Smith called it **"the man of system"** - someone who treats society like chess pieces, forgetting that the pieces *move on their own*.

Limits Are Not the Enemy

So what's the alternative?

It begins with a radical idea:

Limits are not failures. They are features.

Scarcity teaches us to prioritize.
Diversity teaches us to negotiate.
Uncertainty forces us to stay humble and adapt.

Markets, when functioning, embrace these limits:

- They can't solve every problem.
- They can't equalize every outcome.
- They can't make people moral.

But they **create feedback**, reward experimentation, and allow peaceful adjustment. That's not utopia.

But it's better than trying to *force utopia into existence at gunpoint*.

Moral Humility and the Role of Imperfection

Smith and Mises both understood that **humility is the foundation of wisdom.**

Smith saw it in ethics: no man can fully judge another - so we must act in ways that earn mutual respect.

Mises saw it in economics: no planner can fully know another's preferences - so we must allow *each person* to pursue their own ends.

Imperfection is not a sign that the system is broken.

It's a sign that the system is **accounting for human dignity and complexity.**

Perfect equality would require perfect control.
Perfect morality would require thought police.
Perfect fairness would require someone with total power to define fairness.

That's not justice. That's **a velvet cage.**

Building Better - Not Perfect

Rejecting utopia does not mean embracing stagnation.

We can still build:

- Better schools.
- Better policies.
- Better technologies.
- Better laws.
- Better cultures.

But we must do so:

- **Iteratively**, not ideologically.
- **Voluntarily**, not violently.
- **Locally**, not universally.
- **Adaptively**, not rigidly.
- **With humility**, not hubris.

This is what markets do well.
And what moral individuals do best.

Progress is not a leap into heaven.
It's **step-by-step, feedback-driven learning** - in families, firms, towns, and lives.

What You Can Do

In your own life, resist the urge to:

- Cancel everyone who gets it wrong.
- Burn down institutions that aren't perfect.
- Demand purity before participation.
- Chase causes that promise paradise with no cost.

Instead:

- Build systems that get better over time.
- Leave room for disagreement, failure, and growth.
- Honor feedback more than slogans.
- Praise the hard, slow work of reform over the seductive rush of revolution.

Remember:
Utopia doesn't need you to listen.
Reality does.

The Real Goal Isn't Perfection. It's Endurance.

Let me leave you with this:

The best societies are not the most perfect.
They are the most *resilient*.

They bend without breaking.
They adjust without collapsing.
They tolerate mess, because they trust the process.

That process - freedom, cooperation, accountability, choice - is not neat.

But it is *moral*.
And it is *human*.

Smith and Mises both gave us a blueprint - not for heaven on earth, but for a society in which **fallible people can still live with dignity, purpose, and peace.**

Let us choose that world.

Because perfection is a myth.
But liberty - though limited - is *real*.

Chapter 23: Progress Without Permission

Entrepreneurship as Human Flourishing

Think about the last thing that improved your life.

Maybe it was an app that saved you time.
A meal delivery service that made parenting easier.
A podcast that changed your thinking.
A local bakery that made your morning better.

Chances are, it wasn't created by a government department.
It didn't require your vote.
It wasn't handed down from above.

It was the product of **someone's idea, risk, hustle, and insight**.

That's entrepreneurship.

And in a world longing for justice, creativity, and progress, few forces are more powerful than **ordinary people building better solutions - without waiting for permission.**

This chapter is about entrepreneurship as **a moral act**, a civic contribution, and a form of **creative agency** that Adam Smith and Ludwig von Mises both saw as essential to human flourishing.

Because the entrepreneur doesn't just chase profit.

The entrepreneur says:

"Here is a problem - and I think I can solve it."

What Is an Entrepreneur, Really?

Let's define it simply.

An entrepreneur is **anyone who sees a need, imagines a solution, and takes the risk to bring it to life**.

This can be:

- A tech founder in Silicon Valley.
- A food truck owner in Detroit.
- A home-schooling parent who starts a co-op.
- A refugee opening a small tailoring shop.
- A high schooler building an Etsy brand.

Entrepreneurship is not about scale.

It's about **agency**.

Mises called the entrepreneur "the driving force of the market economy." Smith saw traders and craftsmen as vital to both **progress** and **moral development**.

Because in building something new, the entrepreneur also builds **responsibility, connection, and value**.

Why Markets Need Entrepreneurs

Here's the thing about free markets:

They don't evolve through theory. They evolve through *experimentation*.

- You don't know what customers want until someone tries something new.
- You don't know what's possible until someone breaks a pattern.
- You don't improve society by mandating progress - you empower it through action.

Mises emphasized that markets are **not static**. They're in constant motion.

And that motion comes not from central plans, but from **entrepreneurs acting on hunches, passion, or frustration.**

Entrepreneurship is how:

- Old industries get disrupted.
- New problems get solved.
- Marginalized communities build wealth on their own terms.
- Cultures express themselves economically.
- Freedom becomes **visible** in new products, platforms, services, and spaces.

It's not just business.

It's *creation*.

The Moral Case for Entrepreneurship

Let's go deeper.

In a free society, you don't just *have* the right to build something - you have the **moral opportunity** to do so.

Entrepreneurship expresses:

- **Stewardship**: Turning resources into something more useful.
- **Empathy**: Understanding what people need.
- **Courage**: Taking risk without guarantees.
- **Trust**: Relying on strangers to support your idea.
- **Reciprocity**: Earning income by solving others' problems.

Every customer served is a **voluntary affirmation**:
"I see value in what you've made."

Every competitor respects your right to try - even as they try to do better.

Smith saw this as a form of **moral sentiment** in action.
Mises saw it as the ultimate **praxeological proof** that people act with purpose.

Entrepreneurship is not selfishness.

It's **self-direction in the service of others.**

Progress Doesn't Ask for Permission

One of the greatest virtues of entrepreneurship is that it bypasses **gatekeepers**.

- You don't need a government grant to start coding.
- You don't need an Ivy League degree to start a YouTube channel.
- You don't need a boardroom to solve a problem.

In a market society, progress is **permissionless**.

Anyone can:

- Spot a flaw.
- Design a fix.
- Offer it to the world.
- Fail. Adjust. Try again.

That cycle - *build, test, learn* - is how societies **adapt without revolt**.

Entrepreneurs are not just creators of wealth.

They are **pressure valves for change** - ways to respond to injustice, inefficiency, or need without begging the state for reform.

That's moral power.
That's democratic dynamism.

Barriers to Entrepreneurship - and How to Tear Them Down

Despite all this, many people **can't** start businesses easily.

Why?

- **Licensing laws** that require thousands of dollars to braid hair or drive a cab.
- **Zoning restrictions** that prevent home businesses.
- **Tax codes** that punish small firms while rewarding big ones.
- **Banking systems** that exclude minorities or the poor.
- **Cultural gatekeeping** that discourages "non-traditional" entrepreneurs.

These are not market failures.
They are **policy failures** - the very kind Smith and Mises warned about.

If we want justice, we must tear down **barriers to entry**, not build new bureaucracies.

- Let people try.
- Let them fail.
- Let them succeed.

Because **opportunity delayed is prosperity denied.**

Entrepreneurship as Social Mobility

Let's be blunt:

In many societies, entrepreneurship is the only real path out of poverty.

It doesn't require credentials.
It doesn't care about your past.
It doesn't ask where you came from - only what you can *create*.

Smith wrote that upward mobility was moral and admirable - not something to be resented.

Mises believed capitalism "turns luxuries into common goods" precisely because entrepreneurs scale what once was elite.

Think about:

- Smartphones.
- Streaming.
- Rideshares.
- Fast fashion.
- Affordable medicine.

Each was once "for the few." Now they're **for the many.** Because someone found a way to make it *work at scale*.

Entrepreneurs don't just rise. They **lift others.**

Culture, Identity, and Expression Through Enterprise

Entrepreneurship is not just economic.

It's **cultural**.

Through business, people:

- Preserve recipes, rituals, crafts.
- Solve local problems in local ways.
- Speak with *action*, not just protest.

You see this in:

- Black-owned bookstores reclaiming narratives.
- LGBTQ-run cafés creating safe spaces.
- Indigenous artisans reviving ancient designs.
- Women-led fintech startups reimagining credit.

This is not tokenism. It's **creative ownership**.

Entrepreneurship gives people a chance to say:

"This is who we are. And we're offering it to the world."

What You Can Do

You don't need to launch a startup to support entrepreneurship.

You can:

- Buy from small businesses.
- Mentor someone just getting started.
- Vote for deregulation that expands access.
- Teach young people that *they can build something real*.
- Invest - financially or emotionally - in local creators.

And if you feel the itch to try something?

Start.

You don't need perfection. Just a problem to solve and a willingness to try.

Because **freedom means nothing if we don't use it to create.**

The Entrepreneur as Citizen

Smith believed a good life was one of productive purpose.

Mises believed freedom was most visible in people acting to **improve their own condition - and thereby improve society.**

The entrepreneur is the living example.

They:

- Act instead of wait.
- Risk instead of complain.
- Build instead of beg.
- Learn instead of lecture.

They are **builders of prosperity, trust, identity, and change**.

They do not ask for permission.

They act - because the world needs better, and they believe they might help.

Let's never forget:

**The most revolutionary force in the world is not rage.
It is a person with an idea - and the freedom to try it.**

Chapter 24: What Government Is For - and What It Must Never Become

Protecting Liberty Without Becoming Its Master

There's a dangerous myth in politics - shared by both extremists and idealists - that government is either:

- **The enemy of all freedom**,
  - or
- **The savior of all problems.**

But government is neither a villain nor a messiah.

It's a **tool**.

A **necessary framework** - but not a substitute - for culture, conscience, markets, or morality.

Adam Smith and Ludwig von Mises both believed in **limited government**. Not because they were anarchists. But because they understood:

The more powerful the state becomes, the more freedom must shrink to accommodate it.

In this chapter, we'll explore:

- What good government actually *does well.*
- Where it begins to *do harm.*
- And how to **keep it in its place** - as servant, not master.

The Moral Case for Government

Smith and Mises were not utopians. They knew that **government is essential in key ways**:

1. **Protecting Property and Life**

   Laws, courts, and police are necessary to prevent force, fraud, and theft.

2. **Enforcing Contracts**

   Markets don't work without trust. Contracts must be honored and disputes resolved.

3. **National Defense**

   A free society must be defended against external threats.

4. **Certain Public Goods**

   Roads, clean water, and basic public health infrastructure can be hard to fund privately and equitably.

Smith saw these as **public institutions for the common good**. Mises agreed - but added that *every expansion beyond these core tasks* risks **corrupting incentives, suppressing choice, and bloating bureaucracy.**

In short:

The state is needed - but it must be *bound*.

Where Government Goes Wrong

Here's where things unravel.

When government:

- Picks winners and losers in the economy.
- Subsidizes politically favored industries.
- Creates moral laws that coerce private values.
- Uses taxation as punishment rather than revenue.
- Expands roles it cannot do well - and crowds out what people *could* do better.

It becomes a **distortion**, not a safeguard.

This is the heart of Mises's critique:

Every time the state intervenes beyond its proper sphere, it creates secondary effects that often contradict its original intent.

Smith, ever the realist, warned about **regulators being captured by the regulated**, turning public service into **private collusion**.

Government doesn't just cost money.
It can cost **dynamism, innovation, and freedom**.

The Illusion of Benevolent Control

Here's the dangerous temptation:

"If we just had the right leaders, more centralized power could do great things."

But power is **not a neutral tool**.
Even with good intentions, it tends to:

- Drift toward control.
- Expand beyond mandate.
- Resent dissent.
- Reward loyalty over merit.

Government is not run by angels. It is run by *people*.
And those people are subject to:

- Ego.
- Pressure.
- Incentives.
- Bias.

Mises warned: **The state tends to act as if it owns its citizens.**
Smith added: **The larger it gets, the more disconnected it becomes from those it claims to serve.**

The lesson?

Don't empower government to do what you wouldn't trust your opponent to control.

Centralization vs. Governance

There's a difference between **governance** and **centralization**.

- Governance means rules that protect rights, enforce contracts, and ensure fairness.

- Centralization means distant bureaucracies making one-size-fits-all decisions.

Governance is **a framework for liberty**.
Centralization is **an erosion of it**.

Smith believed most decisions should be local - where knowledge is real and consequences are near.

Mises extended this idea, arguing that **decentralization protects diversity and encourages experimentation.**

A country of 300 million should not be governed as if it were a town of 300.

When Government Crowds Out the Citizen

Every time the state expands into new territory, **civil society contracts**.

- When the state replaces charity, communities become less generous.
- When the state replaces parenting, families weaken.
- When the state replaces trade, markets ossify.
- When the state replaces personal risk, entrepreneurship dies.

This isn't always obvious.
It feels like security. Like convenience.

But over time, people forget **how to act freely**.
They stop solving problems.
They stop building.
They stop *owning* their neighborhoods, schools, and lives.

Smith feared this.
Mises called it **dependency disguised as justice.**

And both warned:

A society that forgets how to self-govern will eventually be governed harshly.

How to Limit Government - and Strengthen Society

So what do we do?

1. Demand Clarity of Purpose

Government must have **defined roles** - not vague mandates.

- Protect rights.
- Enforce contracts.
- Defend borders.
- Leave the rest to free individuals and voluntary associations.

2. Insist on Accountability

Every expansion of state power must come with:

- Oversight.
- Sunset clauses.
- Transparency.
- Citizen recourse.

3. Decentralize Wherever Possible

Power should be local.

When decisions are made closer to those affected, outcomes improve - and trust grows.

4. Strengthen Alternatives

Don't just shrink government. **Grow society**.

- Support nonprofits, co-ops, schools of choice, private innovation.
- Invest in families, religious groups, communities, and entrepreneurs.
- Celebrate institutions that work *without coercion*.

What Government Must Never Become

There are three roles government must *never* assume:

1. **The Parent of Adults**

   You are not a child. You don't need to be told what's best "for your own good."

2. **The Morality Police**

   Governments must enforce laws, not legislate personal virtue. Tolerance is a two-way street.

3. **The Economic Planner**

   No government can match the information, flexibility, or creativity of millions of individuals acting freely in the market.

When government becomes any of these, it loses its soul - and eventually, so does the nation.

What You Can Do

You are not powerless.

- Vote with discernment - not for promises, but for boundaries.
- Question the size and scope of every new policy.
- Get involved in local government - where real change often starts.
- Push for sunset laws, audits, and citizen review boards.
- Model self-governance in your own life.

And most of all:

Live in a way that makes less government *necessary*.

Be generous. Be just. Be trustworthy. Build things. Solve problems. Teach others. Lead locally.

Because a free society isn't kept alive by constitutions alone.

It's kept alive by *citizens who don't need to be ruled.*

A Government That Serves - and Stays in Its Lane

Adam Smith saw the state as a **necessary guardian**, not a master craftsman.
Mises believed government must **secure the playing field**, not decide the game.

Let's return to that vision.

Let government be:

- **Strong** where it must be - courts, contracts, protection.
- **Absent** where it should be - commerce, conscience, creativity.
- **Accountable** always - because it holds a sword, not a crown.

When government stays within its moral boundaries, people rise.
And when it doesn't - people shrink.

Let's choose wisely.

Chapter 25: What We Owe Each Other

Liberty, Morality, and the Modern World

You and I have never met.
We might not share a language, a country, a faith, or a lifestyle.

And yet -
When I offer something of value to you…
And you return something of value to me…
We both walk away better.

No threats. No force. No need to agree on everything.

Just **voluntary cooperation**, rooted in **mutual dignity**.

That's what a truly free society looks like.

But for it to last, for it to *work*, something deeper must hold it together:

Not shared identity.
Not centralized planning.
Not mandated unity.

But a set of **moral commitments** we freely embrace - not because they're enforced, but because they're *right*.

This is what Adam Smith and Ludwig von Mises understood better than most:
That liberty, without virtue, cannot endure.
And that morality, without freedom, is not morality at all - it's obedience.

So what do we owe each other?

Let's answer - not with slogans, but with the quiet truths that have shaped every chapter of this book.

1. We Owe Each Other Respect for Agency

Every person is a moral actor.
Not a cog. Not a consumer. Not a demographic.

You have your goals. I have mine.
Freedom means **neither of us has the right to override the other's will -**
except to protect life or property.

This is the foundation of all markets, all contracts, all peace.

- I may not like your choices.
- You may not understand mine.

But we agree on this:

We are both free to try, to fail, to learn, to speak, to build.

That respect is the **price of peace.**

---

2. We Owe Each Other Honesty

Freedom thrives on feedback. But feedback requires **truth.**

- If we lie in business, trust collapses.
- If we deceive in politics, liberty erodes.
- If we fake our intentions, cooperation dies.

Smith believed honesty made sympathy possible.
Mises knew that markets punish dishonesty *eventually* - but that cultures
must still demand it *consistently*.

So we owe each other:

- Truth in trade.
- Truth in speech.
- Truth in motives.

Not because we're perfect. But because **freedom without truth becomes manipulation.**

---

3. We Owe Each Other Tolerance

In a free society, your neighbor will sometimes shock you.

- Their art.
- Their opinions.
- Their decisions.
- Their lifestyle.

But as long as they don't violate your rights, **they don't need your permission.**

Moral progress requires room for **difference** - not just legally, but culturally.

Smith believed morality arose from dialogue and diversity.
Mises knew that progress happens when people **try strange, new, risky things**.

So we owe each other **space to live differently**.

That's not weakness.

It's **strength, matured.**

4. We Owe Each Other Accountability

Freedom is not "do whatever you want."
It's **"do what you choose - and own the consequences."**

This means:

- Businesses should pay the costs of their mistakes.
- Citizens should vote responsibly.
- Parents should raise thoughtful children.
- Communities should face their failures - without scapegoats.

Markets provide some accountability - through prices, reviews, and competition.
Laws provide more - through courts and consequences.

But the most powerful form is **internal**.

Smith called it the "impartial spectator."
Mises called it **rational action.**

We must live with a sense that:

Someone is watching - and that someone is *us*.

---

5. We Owe Each Other the Freedom to Earn, Build, and Rise

It is not enough to protect liberty in theory.

We must **clear the path** so that *others* can use it.

That means:

- Removing barriers to entry.
- Encouraging entrepreneurship.
- Celebrating success earned honestly.
- Opposing systems - public or private - that rig outcomes.

A society where only the already-powerful thrive is not free.

A society where anyone can try, risk, and rise **is.**

Mises believed capitalism made this mobility possible.
Smith believed moral citizens made it *sustainable*.

So we owe each other **opportunity without envy.**

---

6. We Owe Each Other Restraint

Just because you can say something doesn't mean you should.
Just because you can dominate doesn't mean it's moral.

Restraint is **the invisible structure of freedom**.

- Not cheating when you could.
- Not profiting through deception.
- Not crushing competitors through corruption.
- Not speaking hate under the guise of "truth."

Smith believed restraint was trained through community.
Mises believed it was chosen through purpose.

Let us act not just from **rights**, but from **respect**.

---

7. We Owe Each Other Courage

Courage to:

- Disagree without dehumanizing.
- Build something new when the system fails.
- Speak up when freedom is eroded.
- Admit when we were wrong - and grow.

Because freedom is fragile.

And **cowardice is its greatest threat.**

Smith admired the courage to act morally despite ridicule.
Mises warned against "the timid man who dreads responsibility."

We owe each other the courage to be **adults in a free society**.

What Liberty Asks of Us - Now

Liberty is not a guarantee.
It is not a legacy we inherit without effort.

It is **a pattern of living**:

- Trading freely.
- Speaking truthfully.
- Acting honorably.
- Building boldly.
- Governing lightly.
- Loving fiercely.

Smith and Mises left us with no utopias.
But they left us something better:

A world where free people, acting voluntarily, guided by conscience and cooperation, can **create progress that endures.**

Not because they were told to.
But because they *chose* to.

Let us be those people.

The Modern World Needs This

In a time of division, censorship, centralization, and control, we must return to these first principles:

- That trade builds peace.
- That prices reveal value.
- That liberty demands character.
- That government must be restrained.
- That justice starts with honest systems and self-governing people.
- That progress comes not from perfect plans, but from millions of free minds in motion.

And most of all -

That **we owe each other the freedom to try**.

To fail.
To speak.
To love.
To work.
To build.
To disagree.
To rise.

Because what we owe each other is not uniformity.

It is **dignity in difference**.

In Closing

The lessons of Smith and Mises are not just historical.
They are **urgent.**

In a world obsessed with control, we must be **architects of voluntary cooperation**.

In a culture drowning in grievance, we must be **creators of value**.

In a time of institutional failure, we must be **entrepreneurs of trust.**

And above all -
We must be **citizens**. Not of nations alone.
But of a moral order built on freedom, earned respect, and shared hope.

That's what we owe each other.

Let's begin.

Epilogue

The Quiet Work of Freedom

When the last speech has ended,
When the last vote has been cast,
When the headlines fade and the world quiets down -
We are left with the simple, sacred work of being free.

Not in theory.
In practice.

Because freedom is not a one-time gift.
It is a habit.
A discipline.
A relationship.

It must be built, every day, in the mundane choices we make:

- To speak honestly when it would be easier to flatter.
- To trade fairly when no one is watching.
- To allow others to live differently without reaching for control.
- To use our liberty not for indulgence, but for contribution.
- To stand firm when liberty is threatened - not with rage, but with reason.

This is the work that sustains civilization.

Not the grand gesture.
The daily courage.

What we owe each other is not perfection.
It is presence.
Principle.
And the will to remain free *together*, even when we disagree.

Smith and Mises gave us a vocabulary.
Our task is to give it a life.

So let us leave theory now - gratefully, humbly - and return to the marketplace, the home, the community, the vote, the workbench, the screen, the street.

Let us live as people who know:

That freedom is not something you keep by chance.
It is something you keep by choice.

And may we choose well.

Together.

Bibliography

Primary Sources

- Mises, Ludwig von. *Human Action: A Treatise on Economics*. Yale University Press, 1949 (original edition); Liberty Fund, 2007 (Scholars Edition).
- Smith, Adam. *An Inquiry into the Nature and Causes of the Wealth of Nations*. 1776. Edited by Edwin Cannan, Modern Library, 2000.
- Smith, Adam. *The Theory of Moral Sentiments*. 1759. Edited by D.D. Raphael and A.L. Macfie, Liberty Fund, 1982.

Supplementary and Contextual Sources

- Hayek, F.A. *The Road to Serfdom*. University of Chicago Press, 1944.
- Hazlitt, Henry. *Economics in One Lesson*. Harper & Brothers, 1946.
- Friedman, Milton. *Capitalism and Freedom*. University of Chicago Press, 1962.
- Sowell, Thomas. *Basic Economics: A Common Sense Guide to the Economy*. Basic Books, various editions.
- Haidt, Jonathan. *The Righteous Mind: Why Good People Are Divided by Politics and Religion*. Pantheon Books, 2012.
- Bastiat, Frédéric. *The Law*. 1850. Foundation for Economic Education, various editions.
- Nozick, Robert. *Anarchy, State, and Utopia*. Basic Books, 1974.
- Tocqueville, Alexis de. *Democracy in America*. 1835–1840. Translated by Harvey C. Mansfield and Delba Winthrop, University of Chicago Press, 2000.

Modern Economic and Cultural References

- Pinker, Steven. *Enlightenment Now: The Case for Reason, Science, Humanism, and Progress*. Viking, 2018.
- Bregman, Rutger. *Utopia for Realists: How We Can Build the Ideal World*. Little, Brown and Company, 2017.
- McCloskey, Deirdre N. *Bourgeois Equality: How Ideas, Not Capital or Institutions, Enriched the World*. University of Chicago Press, 2016.
- Deneen, Patrick J. *Why Liberalism Failed*. Yale University Press, 2018.

Public Domain and Open-Source Contributions

- Ludwig von Mises Institute. Various open-access publications and essays.
- Liberty Fund. Online Library of Liberty – Primary source hosting and scholarship on Smith, Mises, Bastiat, and Hayek.
- Foundation for Economic Education (FEE.org). Articles and primers on classical liberal economics and voluntary exchange.

Glossary

Agency
The capacity of individuals to make independent choices and act on them. In the context of this book, agency is the foundation of personal responsibility and moral action.

Capitalism
An economic system based on private ownership of the means of production, voluntary exchange, and profit-driven enterprise. Capitalism is viewed here not only as an economic structure but also as a framework for human cooperation and moral choice.

Central Planning
An economic and political system in which decisions about production, investment, and distribution are made by a centralized authority, typically the state. Often contrasted with decentralized, market-based systems.

Character
The set of moral and ethical traits that guide individual behavior. In a free society, character is the internal compass that makes external control less necessary.

Coercion
The use of force, threats, or manipulation to control others' behavior. This book draws a clear line between voluntary cooperation and coercion as the foundation of legitimate action.

Contract
A legally enforceable agreement between parties. Contracts are essential to trust and cooperation in a market economy.

Decentralization
The distribution of power away from a central authority to local or individual levels. Decentralization enhances freedom, flexibility, and responsiveness in both governance and markets.

Entrepreneurship
The act of identifying a need, developing a solution, and taking the risk to bring it to life - often through business. Entrepreneurs are portrayed as civic actors, creators, and stewards of value in a free society.

Externality
A side effect of an economic activity that affects third parties who did not choose to be involved (e.g., pollution). Externalities are discussed as one area where markets may fail and where limited state action may be justified.

Freedom (Liberty)
The ability to act, speak, and live without coercion - bounded by the equal rights of others. This book explores liberty as both a legal condition and a moral discipline.

Government
The institution empowered to create and enforce laws. In this book, the role of government is to protect rights, enforce contracts, and provide essential public order - nothing more.

Incentives
Factors that influence human behavior by offering rewards or punishments. Markets use prices and profit as incentives to coordinate activity and align self-interest with public good.

Inequality
Differences in wealth, income, or opportunity. The book distinguishes between inequality that results from diverse individual choices and unjust inequality that results from coercion, fraud, or exclusion.

Justice
Fairness in how people are treated, especially in terms of rights, access, and responsibility. The book defines justice in terms of equality before the law and protection from coercion - not equality of outcome.

Market
A decentralized network where goods, services, and ideas are exchanged voluntarily. Markets are seen here not just as economic mechanisms but as moral arenas of cooperation and trust.

Moral Sentiments
A term from Adam Smith referring to the internal emotions, instincts, and social feedback that guide moral behavior. These include sympathy, conscience, and the desire for mutual respect.

Praxeology
A term from Ludwig von Mises referring to the study of human action. Praxeology assumes that humans act purposefully to achieve desired ends and is the foundation of Austrian economics.

Property Rights
The legal right to use, control, and exchange property. Property rights are essential for personal freedom, economic coordination, and justice.

Responsibility
The moral obligation to own the consequences of one's actions. In a free society, responsibility is the companion of rights.

Spontaneous Order
A system of organization that emerges naturally from the voluntary actions of individuals rather than from central design. Markets, language, and culture often evolve this way.

Subjective Value
The idea that value is determined by individual preferences and context, not by any objective measure. Central to understanding trade and pricing in a free market.

Tolerance
The willingness to live peacefully with others despite differences in values, beliefs, or behavior. A key ingredient in voluntary cooperation.

Trade-Off
A decision that requires sacrificing one thing to gain another. Recognizing trade-offs is a recurring theme in this book, especially in economics, ethics, and policy-making.

Utopianism

The belief that a perfect society can be engineered, usually through central control. The book critiques utopian thinking as dangerous and detached from human complexity.

Voluntary Cooperation

Interactions and agreements entered into freely and without coercion. The foundation of both market exchanges and moral society.